PUFFIN BOOKS
AKBAR

Kavitha Mandana grew up in parts of the Niligiri hills where telephones and TV did not exist. After an idyllic and undisciplined schooling in Ooty, and a degree in English Literature from Coimbatore, she got into a fairly unliterary career as an advertising copywriter in Bangalore. It took a chaotic six years working with print, TV and radio commercials for her to discover she liked writing and illustrating for kids. She writes regularly in the children's supplement of the *Deccan Herald*. Her work has also appeared in *Chatterbox* and *Toot* magazines. *Tenali Raman* (Puffin) was her first historical novel for kids.

Other books in the *Puffin Lives* series

Akbar

THE MIGHTY EMPEROR

KAVITHA MANDANA

PUFFIN BOOKS

An imprint of Penguin Random House

PUFFIN BOOKS

USA | Canada | UK | Ireland | Australia
New Zealand | India | South Africa | China | Singapore

Puffin Books is part of the Penguin Random House group of companies
whose addresses can be found at global.penguinrandomhouse.com

Published by Penguin Random House India Pvt. Ltd
4th Floor, Capital Tower 1, MG Road,
Gurugram 122 002, Haryana, India

First published in Puffin by Penguin Books India 2010

10 9 8 7 6 5 4 3 2

ISBN 9780143330837

Typeset in Bembo by Eleven Arts, New Delhi

Printed at Manipal Technologies Limited, India

www.penguin.co.in

MIX
Paper | Supporting
responsible forestry
FSC® C043100

Contents

1   Desperados!

On a cold evening in Rajasthan, over 550 years ago, a couple of armed men began getting their horses ready for a long ride into the night. Once the sun set, the desert morphed into a different world. From October onwards, a scorching hot day could turn into a freezing night within hours. Apart from the sharp drop in temperature, the bitingly cold wind blowing across the dunes with no trees to break their intensity, would make eyes water. Yet chilly as it gets, the Thar Desert is one of the driest places in the world, with barely 5–10 millimetres of rain through the entire winter.

The two men wrapped themselves in layers of cloth, hoping to beat the cold that would soon envelop the desert along with the darkness, as they dashed off on a desperate mission. They had to somehow find water. The bedraggled group of refugees that they were travelling with had been on the run for the last few months. They had been forced to abandon their palaces, beautifully laid out gardens and enormous wealth in Lahore, in the Punjab, as the army of Sher Shah and his allies chased them over nearly 1000 km. Miraculously, the group had managed to stay just ahead, and out of the reach of their pursuers.

But the journey had taken its toll. Many had deserted the group. Hundreds had been killed in skirmishes. And even more had died from dehydration in the desert. Horses, that had swept this crowd out of harm's way in the tumultuous Punjab, now dropped dead on their knees in the sands of the Thar.

As the water seekers approached a well, in the fading light they noticed fresh hoof prints in the sand; and in the distance were clouds of dust receding into the horizon. Obviously this oasis had just been visited! Their hopes rose . . . *water, at last!*

But when they peered into the well, they found it filled with sand. The men, driven crazy with thirst, couldn't imagine why anybody would damage a precious water source. But night after night, when the exhausted riders found more wells all filled up with sand, they understood. *This was deliberate, well-planned sabotage.* Obviously they were being watched by enemies. Those ever-present fresh hoof marks around every well they'd approached meant that they were being constantly spied on by Rajputs hostile to them. The desert dwellers' superior knowledge of the region gave them an advantage. As the Rajputs tracked the fleeing Northerners, they harassed them, turning the wells en route into useless mirages.

The refugees were tough, battle-hardened Mughals, originally from the mountains beyond the Hindukush range. They were descendants of the fierce Mongol warriors and empire builders Chengis Khan and Timur the Lame. Even the women among them were quite at ease spending months on horseback, covering hundreds of miles on their sturdy *tipchak* highland horses. But the unsuccessful water-collectors felt especially rotten about returning empty-handed to their camp . . . because a beautiful young queen was travelling with them. She was barely fifteen years old and nine months pregnant.

The birth of a Mughal prince or princess was imminent, but only if they could find water. Otherwise, both mother and child could die in this bleak corner of Hindustan.

A dynasty saved by an elephant

Horsemanship was in every Mughal's blood. Across the steppes of Central Asia, where Babur's family came from, kings and their armies spent more time on horseback than on solid ground. In 1526, when Babur's men fought Ibrahim Lodi's massive army at Panipat, it was the first time the Mughals were facing elephants in battle. Yet their superior weapons and formidable cavalry (horse-mounted soldiers) were able to beat Lodi's army.

In India, the Mughals soon grew to appreciate and value elephants. Babur died only four years after his India conquest. Barely thirteen years after his son Humayun had been on the throne in Delhi, it looked liked the Mughals would have to return to their nomadic lives on horseback because Humayun's army was devastatingly defeated by the Afghan, Sher Shah, at Kanauj. The Mughals had been surrounded and driven towards the river. Thousands jumped in, along with their armour and sank to their death. Humayun himself was saved when he leapt

into the Ganga and one of Babur's old elephants ferried him to safety to the opposite shore—shoeless, crownless but alive. But once across the river, it was back to horses for the Mughals, who then raced all the way to Agra and on to Lahore, evading Sher Shah's army.

2 The Girl Who Refused to be Queen

So how had a queen managed to find herself in such a tight spot? Who *was* she? And who was the king who'd exposed his young wife to such awesome dangers? Well, unlike most queens of those days, who came from royal families, Hamida Banu Begum was a relatively unknown commoner. She was from a Persian family settled in Pat, Sind. And the king she was married to was Humayun, eldest son of Babur, the founder of the Mughal dynasty.

Historical records reveal Hamida as the most reluctant of queens. Even as a fourteen year old, she'd had the gumption to refuse thirty-three-year-old Humayun's marriage proposal with unusual firmness. Nobody can blame poor Hamida for her reluctance. When Humayun proposed to her, he was already a well-known opium addict who had managed to lose everything that his father, Babur, had conquered in Hindustan. That had included Punjab, Delhi, Agra, Bihar and Bengal. Even Humayun's own early daring conquests of the rich ports of Gujarat and the kingdom of Malwa were a waste since he'd lost these territories with equal haste. As winter approached in 1542, Humayun, Babur's chosen heir, had

5

been reduced to a fugitive king without a kingdom. Worse, he had also lost the support of his three brothers, Kamran, Askari and Hindal.

At the time Humayun spotted young Hamida at a party arranged by his stepmother Dildar Begum, he was on the run. After being handed a humiliating defeat by Sher Shah on the banks of the Ganga in Kanauj, Humayun had been chased all the way to Punjab. At Lahore, when he tried to start peace negotiations with Sher Shah, the victorious Afghan replied that he would leave the Mughals in peace only if Humayun vacated Punjab and retreated to Kabul. But Humayun's second brother Kamran, who had inherited the regions around Kabul and Kandhahar, was worried that his currently throneless elder brother would grab *his* kingdom. He made it very clear that Humayun was not welcome in Kabul.

Meanwhile, to show that he meant business, Sher Shah's formidable army had crossed the River Beas in hot pursuit of Humayun and the Mughals holed up in Lahore. Even when faced with the Afghan army, Humayun and his brothers couldn't agree on a joint strategy to fight them. In fact, Humayun's brothers seemed more keen on abandoning this down-and-out 'king'. From Lahore, Kamran returned to Kabul, making it very clear that Humayan was not to follow. Hindal and a cousin, Yadgar, planned to travel south to capture Gujarat and attack Sher Shah from there. Haidar, another cousin who could have been an ally, decided he would try his luck elsewhere, at Kashmir, where he did quite well for himself. So not only was Humayun 'kingdomless', he was also homeless and friendless. And he was already married, many times over! He really had no business proposing marriage, when all he could offer a young bride was a dangerous life on the run.

Hamida, on the other hand, came from a well-respected Persian family, who claimed to be descendants of a famous sage, Ahmad Jani. This meant that her family were Shias while Humayun was a Sunni. Besides, as a beautiful and charming young girl, her prospects must have been good, because when Humayun enquired if she was betrothed to anyone, he was told she had been 'asked for'.

And who was it that had 'asked for' young Hamida? Some believe it was Hindal, Humayun's own headstrong younger brother and son of Dildar Begum. That seems a possibility, because he certainly protested the loudest when his big brother proposed to the fourteen year old. Eventually, when Hamida and Humayun's marriage did get finalized after many ups and downs and with much negotiations and diplomacy, Hindal dropped his plans of conquering Gujarat with cousin Yadgar. Instead he left Sind in a sulk and wandered about the wilds of Afghanistan for years with hermits and dervishes.

After an exhausting forty days, with a number of go-betweens working on the proposal, Hamida finally said yes to Humayun. It must have been an excruciating wait for the poor king. Time was running out for him. Amongst the Mughals, brothers and cousins killed each other over thrones and territory. In Sind, Humayun was on the land of Shah Hussein, a cousin hostile to him. Hussein's family had earlier lost Kabul to Babur, when Babur himself had been a throneless king wandering about Central Asia looking for a kingdom! So Humayun couldn't linger on endlessly waiting for a reply from Hamida since cousin Hussein was getting very nervous.

Nearly fifty years later, when Humayun's sister Gulbadan Begum was in her sixties and had spent many happy years of close friendship with sister-in-law Hamida, she wrote about these forty days in her book, *Humayun-nama*. She reports that once, after being rebuffed by Hamida, a love-struck and determined Humayun visited his stepmother's home and asked Hamida to be sent for. The girl refused to show up, cheekily sending word back that, 'If it is to pay my respects, I was exalted by paying my respects the other day. Why should I come again?' At another time she didn't show up claiming, 'To see kings once is lawful, a second time it is forbidden. I shall not come.' But her wisest reply was to Dildar Begum. When the older lady patiently suggested that in any case Hamida would have to get married some day, so why not to a king, the girl replied, 'Oh yes, I shall marry someone. But he shall be a man whose collar my hand can touch, and not one whose skirt it does not reach.'

All this must have been like rubbing salt in Humayun's many war wounds. But eventually Dildar Begum pacified her son Hindal and convinced Hamida to marry Humayun in September 1541. It was a hurried affair. After Humayun had paid out a dower of Rs 2 lakhs, he couldn't have had much money left for grand

and prolonged festivities. Within days, the couple were on the royal barge, heading towards Humayun's camp near Lohri in Western Sind, in present-day Pakistan.

The *Golden Hind*

A year before Humayun's fortunes sank so low, a boy who would change history was born in Plymouth, England. He had not a drop of royal blood in him, rather, he was the first cousin of a famous pirate. The boy was Francis Drake.

As a young teenager, he went to sea to seek his fortune. All of Europe knew what Asia was slow to discover—that the future lay in who controlled the sea. From a royal family that had only ruled land-locked kingdoms, Humayun had been the first Mughal to set eyes on the sea when he'd captured Gujarat (which he lost soon enough). Christopher Columbus had discovered the sea route to North and South America in 1492 and within a few years the Spanish had colonized parts of these continents and were sending back ships loaded with treasure to Spain. From 1519, all the gold looted from the Aztec (Mexican) empire, along with silver mined in Peru, was shipped back in galleons.

At that time, Spain and Portugal ruled the seas. England's sea power was limited to pirates who picked off unescorted ships. Gradually, Francis Drake got better and better at his job, till he was good enough to request the queen of England for permission to 'travel' further. Under a treaty called the Treaty of Tordesillas, the Pope had literally drawn a line down the middle of the Atlantic Ocean, giving Spain the right to all she found west of this line, and Portugal all that she found east of it.

So with his 'permit' from the queen, Drake began looting Spanish ships. His earliest big haul was when he got a ship carrying back Spain's entire yearly earnings from the mule trade in South America. Loyal to the queen, Drake handed over this loot to England. A few years later, sailing a ship called the *Golden Hind* he captured one of the biggest treasures of all time, the Spanish ship *Cacafuego*, returning across the Pacific from Spain's colony, Philippines. The gold from just that one ship reversed England's economy, paying off debts that the country had been unable to settle for years! Yes, piracy was a good state policy!

This daring pirate was knighted by the queen, and as Sir Francis Drake he sailed the *Golden Hind*, right around the world, one of the first seamen to ever do so.

3 🐘 A Reluctant King

What should have been a honeymoon was really a nightmare for the young bride. More and more noblemen, cousins and allies deserted Humayun. Cousin Yadgar, with whom Humayun hoped to attack Gujarat, looked like he had changed his mind, planning to cross over to the side of their enemy cousin in Sind, Shah Hussein. Poor Humayun was reduced to staying awake at night, keeping watch to prevent his friends from deserting him.

In this bleak arid landscape close to the drylands of western Rajasthan, even food was scarce. The travellers lived off berries for days. Mughal soldiers on the march usually survived by raiding the surroundings. But here there was nothing to raid and live off. The few settlers and nomads in this desolate region fled ahead of the Mughals' arrival. Halfway through this scorching journey, Hamida must have realized she was expecting a child. Did she regret her marriage? How much did she long for the peace of her parents' home in Pat? Was she tempted to desert her hopeless husband? After all, her own brother was travelling with her. Babur's first wife, Aisha, had left him during his years of wandering about Central Asia after losing *his* kingdom, Fergana.

Reluctant as Hamida had been to become queen, she probably was the perfect match for Humayun, who himself had been a reluctant king! Babur, in his autobiography *Babur-nama,* sounds very irritated by Humayun's complete lack of ambition. As a prince, this eldest son of Babur had shown every talent required of a king. When just eighteen years old, he commanded the most important right wing of the Mughal army in Babur's first victory on Indian soil at Ambala, Punjab. Soon after, at the historic battle of Panipat, Humayun fought bravely, again at the head of the right wing, playing a crucial role in beating Ibrahim Lodi's much bigger army. Yet after he'd secured the treasures of the Lodi dynasty for his father and gone back to Badakshan to his role as governor, he wrote to Babur that he wanted to 'retire'! For this prince, battle was more of an adventure. His interests seemed to be in mathematics, astrology, astronomy, mechanics, and unfortunately, wine, women and opium.

As a young emperor, Humayun's finest hour had been at the fort of Champanir. It was right after Babur died. Humayun, in one action-packed year, quelled a rebellion by his cousins; defeated the Afghans in Bihar; and then headed to Gujarat. There angry Afghans, still smarting over the humiliation of Babur's victory at Panipat, had gathered under the flag of Bahadur Shah, ruler of Gujarat, threatening to attack Agra. After convincingly beating Bahadur Shah in battle and driving him into the island of Diu, Humayun marched on into the deep forests of Gujarat, in search of the kingdom's famous treasure, hidden in the impregnable fort at Champanir.

The siege went on for four months. When it seemed as if the siege would never end, one night Humayun personally led about 300 young men on an impossible mission. All sections of the fort were extremely well guarded. But Mughal scouts had found one remote corner that was built directly over a dangerous precipice. It was considered unnecessary to post guards at such a difficult approach. Humayun waited for a dark moonless night, and while his army kept the defenders of Champanir engaged and distracted in battle at the main approaches to the fort, he led his small handpicked unit to that suicidal precipice.

Any noise would have alerted those within the fort and this seemingly mad mission would then have to be aborted. In medieval times, soldiers defending a fort poured boiling hot oil on those caught scaling the walls. Most would fall to their deaths. At night, to illuminate the hidden enemy, burning straw was used. Under such a threat, Humayun and his men began their frightening climb up the fort walls. Inch by inch they silently moved up by driving spikes into the rock for footholds. One wrong step meant dropping hundreds of feet down into the pitch dark ravine. But the outrageous gamble paid off. Silently Humayun's band of soldiers entered Champanir and defeated the local garrison. And the treasure they found was unbelievable.

Generous like his father Babur, Humayun rewarded his men handsomely. Each soldier received all the gold and jewellery that could be piled on to his shield! Even then there were unimaginable quantities left. Yet, just eleven years after being crowned emperor of Hindustan by Babur himself, Humayun found himself minus a throne, a kingdom, without the treasury any ruler needed to run a country and surrounded by enemies.

Out in the wilderness and on the run with Hamida by his side, Humayun received word that King Maldev of Marwar, an adversary of Sher Shah, would offer him refuge. So the ever-dwindling group of refugees plunged into the desert, hoping to reach this promised safe haven. But in the nick of time, Humayun discovered that he had been misled. Maldev had planned to use Humayun as a hostage to be traded with Sher Shah. The dejected group had to hurriedly change course. But they had very few options. To their west was Sind and Kabul, which though governed by their own family, was hostile to them. To the north in Punjab, Sher Shah's generals had taken control. Gujarat lay to the south, with the Afghan ruler Bahadur Shah back on its throne. To the east lay Sher Shah and all his allies. The Mughals, unfortunately, were land warriors, otherwise they could have made a dash to the coast and escaped by ship. But there was no such thing as a Mughal navy. Humayun grasped at the only option left. Rana Prasad, a Rajput chieftain of the remote desert province of Umarkot, had offered to help. So that's where the Mughals headed.

Would Umarkot, too, turn into a mirage that they would have to flee from? The trek to this remote fort, now in Pakistan, was a journey through hell. Humayun's troubles were endless. Hamida's advancing pregnancy added urgency to their tired and slow progress. She needed to be in some place safe to deliver the child.

Personally, Humayun had come down to his last set of clothes. His 'royal retinue' was down to seven weather-beaten horsemen. And even his close friends like Munim Beg and Tardi Beg, who had remained by his side with the greatest reluctance, were in better shape; the 'emperor' had paid a high price for having begged them to stand by him. Humayun had to constantly face their contempt. When he requested Tardi Beg to lend his horse for pregnant Hamida to ride on, the latter churlishly refused. As the refugees reached Umarkot, other problems presented themselves. Humayun had no money for the grand presents one king was expected to give to another. While his own treasury was empty, he knew that Tardi Beg had a lot of money with him. But would he loan Humayun any, considering how ungenerous he had been with his horse?

Humayun's few loyal spies had kept him informed about which of the other travellers had money or precious jewellery hidden with them. Humayun himself, bedraggled as he appeared, also had with him a secret stash of gems and jewels. But he'd obviously decided to keep that safe. He knew that there were many more obstacles ahead of him, and a cache of priceless gems could help him overcome them.

As the Mughals drew closer to Umarkot, Humayun had to act fast. He had no idea what lay ahead of him, but he must have looked back on his life and wondered how he had sunk so low. And he was about to sink even lower. He was about to *steal* from those foolish enough to have remained loyal to him!

In the dead of night, as the ragged group slept, the emperor and his servants turned into thieves. The personal treasures that the Mughal noblemen had carried with them was stolen. This, along with a loan Humayun took from Tardi Beg, allowed him to buy some clothes so that he was fit to present himself as an 'emperor'. He was also able to pay what remained of his 'army' and buy suitably grand presents for Rana Prasad and his family.

They'd reached Umarkot just in time. In a few days, with Hamida lodged in the fort and Humayun camping outside, prince Akbar was born.

Princess Rosebud, who lay buried in the British Museum!

On a warm August day in England in 1870, twenty-eight-year-old Annette Ackroyd travelled from her home in Stourbridge, close to Wales, all the way to London to listen to a foreigner speak. She didn't know that this journey would change her life. The man she listened to with rapt attention was the Bengali Brahmo Samaj activist, Keshub Chandra Sen and his topic was 'Women's education in India'. This was a subject close to Annette's heart. As the daughter of a well-established businessman, she had been very lucky. Hers was a rare family by Victorian England standards that believed strongly in women's education. Annette enjoyed the best

opportunities a woman of her time could, at Bedford College, London.

Annette was now ready for a bigger challenge in life. And Keshub Chandra's fiery speech at the Victoria Discussion Society that August, calling his good 'sisters' in England to come to India to educate Indian women, seemed to be just what she was waiting for. Wealthy in her own right, Annette immediately sailed to India.

Unfortunately, things didn't go as smoothly as she'd imagined in Bengal. For one, she found that back in India, Keshub Chandra Sen was rather conservative, quite different from the rousing radical speaker she'd been inspired by in London. He was more inclined to 'educate' women on how to be 'good wives' and daughters, while Annette's idea of education was to give women access to the sciences, mathematics, philosophy, and just about everything a man could learn.

In 1873, she started a school with her own funds, the Hindu Mahila Bidyashala. Though she did get some support from the more liberal thinkers amongst the Bramho Samaj, she found 'women's education' an uphill task and gave up on running her school.

She met and married Henry Beveridge, an ICS (Indian Civil Services) officer. Over the following years, she concentrated on bringing up her four children and learning Turki and Persian.

At this time, much of Mughal history was already well-known. A number of Persian texts like *Babur-nama* and *Akbar-nama* had been translated into English, and a vast number of Persian, Urdu, Turki and Hindi manuscripts had flowed from the libraries of Indian rulers into English hands. But these were all books by men—Babur's very entertaining personal memoir, Akbar's biography written by a dutiful courtier who praised the emperor incessantly. But since Mughal women rarely stepped out in public, nobody knew what *their* lives had been like.

That was until 1901. Luckily for us, a Colonel G.W. Hamilton had spent his years in India collecting manuscripts. When he returned to England and died, his widow sold his collection of over 1000 manuscripts, many of them to the British Museum.

It was among these manuscripts that Annette Beveridge found a rather tattered copy called *Ahwal Humayun Padshah Jamah Kardom Gulbadan Begum bint Babur Padshah amma Akbar Padshah*. Annette soon realized with great excitement that she was reading the book of an aristocratic, extremely well-educated Mughal woman, written over 300 years ago. Not only was it the first account of life in a Mughal zenana, the author also happened to be someone very close to three generations of Mughal emperors. She was Babur's daughter, Humayun's sister and Akbar's very beloved aunt! Annette Beveridge had discovered Gulbadan Begum, whom she fondly referred to as Princess Rosebud. This book with the extra-long title came to be known as the *Humayun-nama*. Unfortunately, the last chapters of the book were missing. It ended about four years before Humayun's death. It was written only because Akbar had cajoled Gulbadan Begum to do so. He wanted a sort of record of all things that she had personally witnessed for Abul Fazl,

his own historian, to read before he embarked on writing the *Akbar-nama*.

Annette Beveridge's translation was completed in 1902, and changed the world's perception of life in a Mughal court.

4 🐘 The Gypsy Prince

When Hamida's labour pains began, the astrologers went into a huddle. The Muslims and Hindus of the medieval world were great believers in the stars, Humayun himself being a well-known practitioner. So as the child's possible date of birth approached, everybody worked overtime drawing up horoscopes. There was great excitement both within the fort and out at the men's camp because, according to the stars, if the child was born during a particular period of the day, it would grow up to be a great person, a world leader whose name would go down in history. But the child seemed determined to show up before that time, ruining its chances of greatness!

Just when it seemed that the baby would be born too early for a good horoscope, a midwife appeared on the scene to help Hamida through the birth. She apparently looked so fierce and threatening, that the young queen recoiled in fright. That jolt set back the whole process by a few hours, so baby Akbar managed to enter this world at the astrologically perfect time!

The birth of a prince in medieval India was usually followed by grand celebrations. Courtiers and family members were showered with expensive gifts and state holidays were declared as the whole country rejoiced. Akbar's birth certainly lifted the flagging spirits of the

Mughals. But the celebrations were muted. Camped out in the wilderness when the news of Akbar's safe delivery reached him, Humayun could only enjoy a quiet moment of thanksgiving. He broke a musk pod, and as the fragrance wafted all over the camp, the new father hoped his son's fame would similarly spread across the world. The same evening, he moved camp, travelling towards Sind.

Even the newborn prince enjoyed just a few weeks of safety. Soon Hamida had to leave the comfort of Umarkot and move on to join her husband, who had set up temporary court while camped in a garden in Jun, Sind. In the fluctuating fortunes of Humayun's life, Jun proved to be a lucky place—for a while. A number of undecided Mughals arrived to show support to him, along with Rajput allies. It seemed that Humayun had actually managed to raise an army of 15,000. But his stature at this point was so diminished that he couldn't unite this motley band of fighters, who each had a separate plan. It didn't require a battle for the poor king to quickly lose his new-found army. Without a sword raised or a shot fired, but with petty in-fighting and quarrelling between the men, this 'army' disbanded! Humayun was now more vulnerable than ever since he was camped in his hostile cousin's territory, and had a baby prince travelling with him.

The dejected, confused and totally directionless wanderings of this bunch of royal gypsies finally ended with the almost magical appearance of the Mughal army's most famous general, Biram Khan. Years ago, when Babur had allied with the Shah of Persia to fight against the Uzbegs in Central Asia, he had met Biram Khan, a Turk in the Persian army. Babur had been so impressed by this well-mannered but brilliant captain that he offered him a good job with the Mughals. And unlike the innumerable cousins, 'allies' and others who kept switching loyalties between the Afghans, Rajputs and the four sons of Babur, Biram Khan's loyalty was unquestionable. He convinced Humayun that hanging around in Sind was pointless. The group would try their luck in Persia, but they first had to cross vast tracts of enemy territory. And beyond lay the mountains which they were going to cross in the dead of winter. Would the baby survive this crazy life on the run?

A melting pot

Hindustan, at this time, was a paradise for the soldier of fortune—someone who is today called a mercenary. Immigrants poured in as news spread across the Middle East about new armies being raised by new dynasties; about kingdoms to be won with ease; and about the country's riches ready to be looted.

While Babur was of Mongol stock from Central Asia, across the Muslim world Persians were considered the most well-educated and cultured. So the best administrative jobs went to Persian scholars who migrated to India. Turkey, under the Ottoman dynasty, controlled vast territory that stretched into Europe and North Africa.

The Turks were considered well ahead in warfare, arms and ammunition. So many local rulers hired Turks to fill senior military posts.

Just as Mughal siblings later won their right to the throne by killing off their brothers and nephews, in Turkey too a young prince, doomed to die in the hands of his elder brother, escaped. He reached India, worked his way up as a commander and eventually founded the Adil Shahi dynasty in the Deccan.

These mercenaries were hired by both Hindu and Muslim rulers. Many Hindu armies had battalions of foreigners, especially to handle the firearms.

5 🐘 A Baby in the Battlefield

Just a few months after surviving the hellish heat of the Thar desert, Hamida Begum, with baby Akbar beside her, now found herself battling sub-zero temperatures. The small group had managed to cross Sind after Biram Khan had negotiated Humayun's safe passage through the country. But their greatest danger was in trying to cross the region around Kandahar to reach the mountains because brothers Kamran, Askari and Hindal were lying in wait. Humayun had written to the Shah of Persia, asking for his help, but the situation was so dangerous that he didn't wait for his reply and kept moving.

The biting wind froze the food even as it was being eaten. Finding anything to eat was itself turning into a losing battle. Hamida had only two women accompanying her, and the forty ragged men who made up the rest of the group could hardly protect her and her newborn, in case of an attack.

One day, while the refugees were camped close to the mountains, a rider came dashing back to the few weather-beaten tents clustered around a struggling fire. He'd spotted an armed gang approaching. Instinctively, Humayun knew it was one of his brothers. He and Hamida had to make a decision within seconds. With absolutely no supplies, baby Akbar would probably not survive the treacherous mountain crossing. Should they risk leaving him behind … with the prayer that whatever the rivalry between the brothers, the uncles would take care of their little nephew?

Young Hamida's heart must have broken when she and her husband rode out of camp leaving Akbar behind in the care of a few trusted family retainers. Would she ever see her first born again?

Moments after the 'king' and 'queen' fled, Askari and his heavily armed gang of men barged into the camp. He claimed he had only come to pay his respects and attend to his elder brother. But nobody was fooled. Yet Humayun's frightful gamble paid off. This fierce prince who'd set out from Kandahar armed for battle and determined to destroy his eldest brother, took one look at his infant nephew and his heart melted! Carrying baby Akbar in his arms, Askari took him back to Kandahar and handed the infant over to his wife Sultanum Begum. Even as a baby, Akbar seemed to have had incredible charm, because she was just one of a long string of foster mothers who took care of Akbar through his chaotic childhood. Each of these women treated him like her own son.

How Akbar survived the constant battles between his father and uncles is a miracle, because he was always in the midst of all the action. A year later, Humayun returned from Persia, having enjoyed a grand reception from the Shah. Now he approached Afghanistan from the west and at the head of a large well-armed Persian army. One of the reasons the Shah had allied with Humayun was because the latter had promised to wrest

Kandahar from his brothers and hand it over to the Persians. As Humayun advanced to Kandahar, Akbar was shifted to Kabul and moved into the care of his grand aunt, Babur's elder sister, Khanzada Begum. Once again, he was looked after with the greatest of love and affection.

When Kandahar fell to Humayun, the ever fickle brothers deserted Kamran and moved on to his side. So as Humayun approached Kabul with his Persian forces, he had brothers Hindal and Askari, sworn enemies of the previous year, as his allies! Kamran fled Kabul and Humayun entered the city as the victor. Most important, he was reunited with his now three-year-old son, Akbar.

For a brief period, before things started hotting up again between the brothers, the first family of the Mughals enjoyed a pleasant reunion. Hamida travelled from Kandahar to Kabul and within weeks Akbar's circumcision ceremony was arranged. Strangely, for all the wars fought between the brothers over territory and throne, the Chugtai clan were very close knit. Powerful and affectionate relationships bound aunts, sisters, mothers and the many wives to all the four brothers, so the brief moments of peace were happy times for the extended family.

But peace was always temporary. Poor Humayun felt bound by a promise he'd made to his father on his death bed about never harming his brothers however much they provoked him. So, unique amongst Mughal princes, he forgave every brotherly betrayal. The result of this was he spent most of his energy fighting his brothers rather than other kings. The battle for the control of Kabul got more intense. Every time Humayun took the city, there would be a brief victory celebration before Kamran would grab it back. The city changed hands five times over a period of ten years. Humayun almost lost his life during these vicious battles and once very nearly lost little Akbar.

It was one of those times when Kamran had occupied the city, with big brother Humayun attacking from outside the fort walls. Humayun was in a very vulnerable position because Kamran had Humayun's family within the fort as hostage. When the battle seemed to be going in favour of Humayun, the desperate Kamran began tossing people over the fort walls. Many children and women from Humayun's side died this way. In the heat of this ugly battle, Humayun froze. From the ramparts of the fort he saw his little son Akbar. The boy was being dangled dangerously over the walls, right in the path of enemy fire. Just in time, Humayun ordered his soldiers to stop firing. Somehow, in spite of Kamran holding Akbar hostage, Humayun went on to win the city. But it was sheer good luck that saved little Akbar's life.

Eventually, peace was achieved within the family only after paying a very heavy price. Mughal advisors came down heavily on Humayun. If he wanted to keep brotherly relations, he needed to step down and abdicate the throne in favour of Kamran. Otherwise he needed to kill Kamran, who had over the last twenty-five years repeatedly betrayed his elder brother. He needed to be treated like a traitor. As Humayun dithered, Kamran killed Hindal in a midnight fight. And Askari, having committed yet another traitorous act, had been asked to make a pilgrimage to Mecca—the polite way for one royal brother to tell another to 'Get lost!' Unable to have his brother killed, Humayun ordered him to be blinded. And only after that, peace reigned.

Buying an army with a diamond!

Even when wily Humayun was down and out roaming in the Rajasthan desert, reduced to stealing the money off his courtiers, he had one ace up his sleeve—a priceless cache of gems. One of these is believed to have been the gorgeous Kohinoor diamond.

After Babur's win at Panipat, it was Humayun who rode on to Agra to secure the Lodi treasury from looters. Apart from immense treasure, he was also surprised to find the Rajput womenfolk of the Gwalior royal family trapped in the city, at the mercy of rampaging mobs. The chivalrous prince immediately offered them protection. For this act he became the rakhi brother of the princess whose father had just died at Panipat (as an ally of Ibrahim Lodi). The grateful family gifted him a tray heaped with the most priceless jewels.

Humayun dutifully handed over these goodies to Babur, who gifted the entire lot, including the spectacular Kohinoor, back to his son. Babur wrote in his memoirs that he believed the stone could pay to feed the entire world, for a couple of days. In any case, when Humayun fled India and sought the Shah of Persia's help against his brothers, he gifted the Kohinoor to the Shah. It was rumoured to be four times the cost of the military aid the Shah gave Humayun.

6 The Boy Who Hated His Books

Prince Akbar was missing! The palace was searched thoroughly, but there was no sign of him. His family, far from worrying too much, merely sent out guards and soldiers to look for him in the fields and hills beyond the city of Kabul. They knew that if he wasn't up to mischief in the palace, he'd be riding some horse bareback, or wrestling with boys much older than him, because that's what he did during his study hour! The moment his very learned and specially selected tutor arrived at the palace, Akbar vanished. He bunked class! And he did so all the time.

Humayun, himself an astronomer and an astrologer, had taken great pains to check for the astrologically prescribed auspicious hour to begin Akbar's formal education. The Mughals were all passionate scholars. Akbar's grandfather Babur was a very well-regarded poet who wrote books in Persian and Turki (the language of the region around present day Turkmenistan and not to be confused with what was spoken in faraway Turkey). Babur's love for books was legendary. While most medieval kings sent spies out to check what gems, jewellery and other treasures could be looted from a country after a war, Babur kept track of what books he could acquire from the libraries of those he defeated! Since the printing press hadn't made its appearance in the East, all manuscripts were painstakingly handwritten in exquisite calligraphy, and so were naturally rare and precious.

Humayun too was obsessed with his library. In the years following his return to Afghanistan after his Persian trip, Kabul had changed hands between Humayun and Kamran a number of times. On one of those occasions when Humayun learnt that his brother had brutally taken over the city, his first question was if Kamran had spared his precious library! Humayun's interests were different from his poetic father's. He was a man of science who loved mathematics, astronomy and mechanics. He had a number of inventions to his credit. How he managed this amid all his constant wanderings is a mystery. He designed a prefabricated, easy-to-transport bridge that the Mughals used on their extensive travels. He even designed and built a floating palace, along with a beautiful garden!

The curriculum of a Mughal prince was very vast; much, much more than what children of today study. The Chugtai princes had to learn Turki, the mother tongue of those whose home land was Fergana (present day Khirgistan). Persian was the language of the court. And Arabic had to be studied to read the Koran. Besides that (with fathers, grandfathers, and even mothers and aunts who composed poetry, practised calligraphy and invented machinery), a prince's syllabus also included mathematics, handwriting, grammar, the sciences, the history of warfare, and a whole lot more. And this was just the 'indoor syllabus'! Princes were expected to be excellent sportsmen too. They had to excel in horse riding, marksmanship, elephant riding, wrestling, swimming and be able to handle a range of weapons like swords and guns.

Just before Akbar was born in a desolate corner of Rajasthan, the chief astrologer had said, 'In a short while, a glorious time will arrive such that will not arrive in a thousand years.' Akbar did arrive at that precise 'glorious time' and eventually lived to be a king that only comes along once in a thousand years, proving that old astrologer right. But when it came to figuring out the auspicious moment for Akbar's book learning to start, no astrologer seemed to get the time right. Poor Humayun tried to restart Akbar's 'education' with four specially selected tutors, at four different 'auspicious hours'. None worked. Finally, Humayun even tried picking tutors by lots. But no amount of fresh auspicious beginnings, persuasion, cajoling and sternness could get Akbar to sit at his books. He was a child built for the outdoors, roaming the countryside hunting and playing fierce competitive games. Akbar never learnt to read and write all his life! He could barely sign his name.

But there were some successes. Akbar loved his painting class. This was one tutor who never had to go looking for his pupil, because Akbar always showed up. In fact, years later, when Akbar was emperor of India, he established one of the best art studios in the world. Painters from all over Central Asia, West Asia and India flocked to Akbar's court because they knew this particular king loved art.

After Humayun had given up in exasperation and Akbar was put under the care of the general Biram Khan, the prince was introduced to yet another tutor, Abdul Latif. This scholar seemed to realize that Akbar had a problem with the written word, so he recited Sufi poetry to the young boy. Surprisingly, Akbar enjoyed this tremendously. Those early recitations of poetry from a liberal branch of Islam must have influenced the young Akbar's views on religion.

A passion for learning

When the Greek and Roman empires of the pre-Christian era faded into oblivion, knowledge found a new home in the Arab world. Christianity had become the religion of Western Europe, with the Pope in Rome as the spiritual leader. Any book that contradicted the Bible's version of 'Creation' was banned. Europe went through a period called the Dark Ages, where the Church actively discouraged any scientific learning. Galileo, the Italian astronomer and scientist, spent the last years of his life under house arrest for having published a book that said that the earth revolved around the sun, rather than the other way round!

Luckily, the Greek classics had been translated into Arabic, and all over the Middle East books on science, mathematics and philosophy filled libraries as Arabic scholars moved forward in scientific exploration. They built further on the learning from ancient Egypt, Greece, China and India. The meteoric rise of Islam was directly

linked to the region's passion for learning. Turkish, Mughal, Arab and Persian rulers were able to conquer unprecedented swathes of land because technologically they were far ahead of those whom they invaded. They had science on their side.

For two centuries after the Ottoman Turks broke the Eastern Roman Empire at Constantinople in the early 1500s, they were far ahead of Europe in firearms, naval technology and military strategy. Similarly, Babur's tiny force of 20,000 Mughal soldiers were able to defeat Ibrahim Lodi's formidable army of 1,00,000 (including 1000 elephants) at Panipat because of his advanced weaponry. Babur was the first in India to use a regiment of musketeers in battle. And with a council of war veterans who had fought in Persian, Turkish and Uzbeg battles, he was able to draw on a rich tradition of inventive war tactics that ultimately proved superior to Lodi's 1,00,000 troops.

Apart from the sciences and literature, knowledge of the Koran was very important. By the age of four or five years, young Muslims were expected to start learning to read and write verses from their holy book at Koranic schools called Kuttabs. When children crossed the 55th chapter, the Surah or al-Rahman, the teacher was honoured with a sheep as gift. Another sheep would be sacrificed at the ceremony called Nafas-ar-rahman (the infusion of the Breath of the Holy One), that was held for the child who has crossed a milestone in Islamic learning. Sheep played another role in education. It was burnt wool mixed with water that made up the ink used for calligraphy. When children learnt to write verses from the Koran elegantly on their *lawh* (a wooden tablet smeared with a white lime mixture, much like a slate), it would be sent home for the parents to appreciate.

With such high standards of learning expected of children, Akbar's absolute refusal to read or write must have devastated his scholarly father.

7   A Crash Course in the School of Life

For a boy who'd spent the first twelve winters of his life in freezing, snow-bound Afghanistan, Akbar's first winter in Punjab was glorious. His father's army had defeated the descendants of Sher Shah and north India was once again back in Mughal hands after fifteen years. The river Sutlej offered the daring prince wonderful opportunities to swim. While an Afghan winter placed a number of restrictions on a child who loved the outdoors, in Punjab he could hunt with dogs, race horses, fly pigeons and generally roam the hills, his curious mind exploring this new territory. After a series of dramatic wins over Sikhandar Shah (Sher Shah's nephew) across the Punjab, the morale of the Mughal soldiers at the camp was high. There was plenty of time for sport—wrestling with the tough prince, playing polo with him or testing their shooting skills against his. Life couldn't have been better for Akbar.

While his father was at Delhi, setting up the new administration and taking a much-needed break from constant fighting, Akbar was only too happy to remain in Punjab, under the care of his guardian, Biram Khan. There was another reason why this contingent of Mughals remained in Punjab. A famine was raging across the plains of India, so in case things didn't go too well for Humayun in Delhi, at least Akbar, his heir, would be safe.

But Akbar's carefree days were soon interrupted. A secret message arrived from Delhi with devastating news—Humayun had died. He had fallen down the stairs one evening after spending time on the terrace doing what he loved best—star gazing. Thirteen-year-old Akbar is reported to have broken down and wept. But young princes of those turbulent times did not have the luxury of even grieving for their parents. At that moment, the most important task for Biram Khan was to keep Humayun's death a secret. Otherwise the recently defeated Afghans would use the opportunity to regroup and take back Delhi. So after only that momentary private breakdown, the young Akbar had to present a bold face in public. He obviously did a good job of hiding his grief, because no one in the Mughal camp in Punjab got to know that the emperor, the boy's father, had died.

The silence continued till Biram Khan was able to ensure that the throne for Akbar was secure. In Delhi, a Humayun look-alike was dressed up every day for two weeks to show his face at the jharoka, the royal balcony from where kings held their public audiences. Almost two weeks after Humayun's death the announcement was finally made to the public. Biram Khan had a makeshift throne built out of bricks and masonry in a garden beside the river Ravi, at Kalanaur, and Akbar was formally made king. The boy who had just entered his teens, was in no way ready for this huge responsibility. But he always had good fortune on his side. And from

14 February 1556, when he became king, his luckiest break was that he had Biram Khan as his guardian.

Years later, when Abul Fazl, Akbar's friend, courtier and carefully picked biographer, was writing about his king's childhood, he justified Akbar's youthful distaste for books and absolute love for games. He wrote that even as a prince, Akbar used sport to understand human nature better without people realizing that they were being observed. Akbar had the unique opportunity to study humans under the most difficult times. As a one year old, he'd been left by his fugitive parents up in the mountains of Afghanistan. As a three year old, an uncle whom he loved had dangled him over the fort walls of Kabul, right in the face of enemy fire. He'd witnessed his family members being thrown down high walls to their death as his father fought his uncles. He'd known that his father had been forced to blind one uncle, and banish another.

Difficulties apart, he had also witnessed some fabulous victories. He'd been very much a part of his father's dramatic recovery of Indian territory. As a mere twelve year old, with his younger brother Mohammed Hakim left behind as governor of Kabul, he accompanied Humayun to Punjab. There he had watched first hand as a paltry contingent of 5,000 Mughals had taken on and spectacularly defeated a 30,000-strong Afghan army. Every subsequent Mughal victory had been won against immensely larger armies. Yes, Akbar had learnt more important lessons in his short life than any tutor could have taught him—about the worst and the best that was possible.

Meanwhile, in faraway England

Akbar's contemporary and counterpart in England was a woman. And she too, initially, sat on a very wobbly throne. But over a period of almost half a century, this young queen who nobody expected to last even a few years, turned her reign into what is called the Golden Age of England. She was Queen Elizabeth I. Before her reign, England had been only a minor European power. Spain and Portugal with their impressive fleets of ships, and gold-rich colonies in South America, were the superpowers.

There were many similarities between Mughal Hindustan and Elizabethan England. Criminals of Akbar's time often had hands chopped off, were thrown into dungeons, and if the crime was plotting against the emperor, the traitor was beheaded, the chopped-off head often displayed as a warning to others. So was the case in England. In London, those approaching one end of the London Bridge were greeted with the grisly sight of the severed heads of those who had been publicly beheaded. In one famous case, a nobleman, Babington, who had plotted to assassinate the Queen, was publicly disembowelled (had his stomach ripped open) while he was still conscious.

When famine struck northern Hindustan, as it often did, most foreign travellers wrote with shock about how removed the royal families were from the poor man's suffering. Yet European royalty, too, lived exactly the same way. Through the sixteenth century, as London was swept by the plague almost every ten years, the royal family just moved out of the city to one of their many palaces across

the British Isles. The common man had to face the horrors of the plague pretty much on his own.

At the end of Elizabeth's 'Golden Age', a series of bad harvests, repeated outbreaks of plague and innumerable naval expeditions had impoverished England. Daily wages for the poorest Englishman was half what it had been a century ago, yet prices were high. In this climate of mounting unemployment, the rich were able to exploit the poor even further. When one great landowner, Sir Thomas Gresham, discovered that he'd get better returns on his farm land if he left it as grazing land, he promptly turned out the hundreds of poor tenant farmers from his vast properties. Most of them were instantly turned into beggars, while he became England's richest commoner.

In 1604, the year after James the First succeeded to the throne on Elizabeth's death, in one year alone he spent over 22 million pounds in today's value, on personal jewellery. No, there was not much difference between the Oriental Despot and his Western counterpart!

Normally, in Europe, the eldest son was considered heir to the throne. The dreadful wars of succession that India witnessed between the Mughal siblings were not normal in the West. But poor Queen Elizabeth found herself in an awkward, 'Oriental despot-like' situation. Her father, Henry VIII, had six wives (often murdering one to marry the next), so there were many aspirants to the throne. The Roman Catholic Church did not permit more than one wife, even to a king, and did not allow divorce. So Henry took the easy way out and broke off from the Catholic Church before going on to marry his six wives! England then became Protestant, a less ritualistic branch of Christianity that had evolved in Germany 'in protest' against the very elaborate Roman Catholic Church. Consequently, Elizabeth not only had to deal with other stepsisters and brothers, but also with a furious and powerful Pope, the head of the Catholic Church, who wanted England to return to being a Catholic state, loyal to Rome.

Right through her reign, powerful Catholic kingdoms in Europe tried to topple the Protestant Elizabeth and put her Catholic stepsister, Mary Queen of Scots, on the throne. Finally, Elizabeth had her sister beheaded in the Tower of London in 1587—just as many a Mughal ruler had done to secure his throne.

8 A Night of Bad Dreams

In a camp around Panipat in November 1556, a tightly packed group of warriors jostled about as they tried to peer over each other's heads to watch a lone man gorge himself on mutton. His appetite seemed insatiable. Like a maniac, he ripped the flesh off the bones. The tension in the audience was palpable. Everyone stopped breathing when the man finally found what he was looking for—the blade bone of the slaughtered sheep. In a trance, he stared at it, 'reading' it like a sign board. His long silence and his crazed expression drove the crowd close to breaking point and then, finally, his lips began to move. This was Ahmad Beg, the crazy fortune teller, who never got it wrong.

Finally, he made his announcement. The Mughals would win . . . decisively! A wild cheer went up from those who'd been watching nervously.

★ ★ ★

The Mughals' second entry into India had been deceptively easy. Sher Shah had died and his nephews were in battle with each other. So Humayun had no trouble re-conquering the lost Mughal lands from the Afghans. But with Humayun's death, Hindustan was once again up for grabs. Everybody wanted to take advantage of the young Akbar's inexperience. So within just a few months of being crowned king, Akbar lost Agra, the capital of his kingdom.

The trouble had started in Bihar. Sher Shah's grandson had been murdered while still an infant by the boy's maternal uncle, Adil Shah. But this power grabber was more interested in dance and music than in administering territories. He had left that job in the able hands of his military commander, Hemu.

Hemu had risen from being a small trader. Somehow he'd caught the attention of Adil Shah, who made him the overseer of the Delhi market and from there he managed a career shift to Head of Intelligence. Soon he took over all the military campaigns of the Bihar branch of the Sur dynasty, in which he performed spectacularly.

In the run up to the Second Battle of Panipat against Akbar, Hemu had led the Afghan army to over twenty-two successive victories. He'd driven the Mughal governor out of Gwalior; audaciously attacked the Mughal capital, Agra and chased the veteran warrior Iskander Khan Uzbeg and his troops out of the city; he then marched on to Delhi, and defeated the combined forces of the fleeing Iskander Khan Uzbeg and Tardi Beg. Once there, he almost forgot that he was an officer in the army of Adil Shah. He minted coins in his own name and called himself Raja Vikramaditya.

All the great Mughal generals fled to Punjab, where Akbar and Biram Khan were stationed, waiting to escort the women of the Mughal royal family into India for the first time. Biram Khan decided that Hemu had to be stopped. Instead of fleeing to Kabul as some veterans wanted, he got Akbar ready for his first battle as a king. The battlefield was to be at Panipat, where Akbar's grandfather, Babur, had scripted an amazing victory.

While the message in the sheep bone had promised the Mughals a victory, on the Afghan side the omens were bad. Right at Adil Shah's court itself, the astrologers had advised Hemu to avoid attacking Akbar, because the young king's horoscope was very powerful. But Hemu persisted. Yet, just before the battle, this unbeatable military commander had a bad dream. He saw his elephant drown and himself pulled to safety by the Mughals. The following day, a favourite elephant of Hemu's was actually struck dead by lightning. But Hemu was determined to go to battle.

That November at Panipat, Hemu's brilliant strategies almost proved both the sheep-bone prophecy and his bad dream wrong. Almost. But just when an Afghan victory seemed certain, an arrow pierced Hemu's eye, knocking him down from his war elephant Hawai. Within minutes the Afghan army was in disarray. The Mughals quickly captured Hemu and Biram Khan himself beheaded him. Akbar's good luck had won the battle!

With the defeat of Hemu, the Mughals won back Gwalior, Delhi and Agra.

Misreading the stars

Love of astrology and astronomy proved to be the death of Humayun. After his reconquest of Hindustan, Humayun had retired for a while from his hectic military activity to set up his library and observatory at Delhi. He'd chosen one of Sher Shah's mansions for the purpose. On 24 January 1556, Humayun believed Venus rising in the night sky was especially auspicious and decided to watch it with his friends. Returning downstairs from the roof-top pavilion, he tripped and fell down the staircase, injuring his head. Within a few days, he was dead.

So, in a sense, Sher Shah *did* eventually manage to get Humayun . . . even if it was long after the Afghan's own death!

9 A Tug of War

Hunting was a passion with Akbar. So no one looked too closely at the eighteen-year-old king as he got ready to leave the Agra palace on a shikar. If anyone's suspicions had been aroused, they might have noticed that the crowd accompanying him was a bit larger than necessary; that the group carried more luggage than shikaris normally did; and that his foster mother, Maham Anaga, suddenly seemed to have taken a great interest in hunting.

After the 'hunters' were well out of range of those who might have been spying from the ramparts of the fort, they changed course. Instead of heading off into the nearby jungles, they began a mad race to Delhi, a distance of over 250 km.

Akbar was running away from his foster father and guardian, Biram Khan. And the person who had helped him plot the entire escapade was his foster mother, Maham Anaga.

★ ★ ★

When Humayun died, Akbar was alone in Punjab with the man his father had appointed as his guardian, Biram Khan. That had been a close relationship. Akbar even called his guardian 'Khan Baba'. As a thirteen year old, his life depended on Khan Baba. If as guardian or regent, Biram Khan had been less capable, Akbar could have lost either his throne, his life, or both, in the tussle for power between the Chugtai cousins, uncles and other senior generals. But Biram Khan's fierce loyalty to the family and his immense talents as an administrator and commander, kept the throne safe for Akbar.

But while a thirteen year old who had just lost his father might have accepted all that Biram Khan ordered him to do, at eighteen, Akbar began to rebel. Now nearly an adult, he probably wanted to shake off Biram Khan's control over his life. Also, Akbar's mother, Hamida Banu Begum was close at hand in Delhi, while his beloved foster mother was part of the zenana at Agra, so the young king had others to lean on.

When Akbar rebelled against Biram Khan's lectures on cost-cutting, he had his foster mother to grumble to. When Biram Khan objected to Akbar taking a second wife immediately after his first marriage, the young king had support from the women in his family.

The more powerful and strong the Mughal empire became, the more jealousy Biram Khan attracted. One factor that contributed to a rift amongst courtiers was that the Chugtai family were Sunni Muslims from Central Asia, while Biram Khan was a Shia from Turkey. When he appointed a Shia as the Head of the Department of Religion, there was much anger amongst the Sunnis, especially among the women in the harem.

In 1560, Akbar confided his wish to break free from his foster father to Maham Anaga, who seized the opportunity to wean away the king from this influential figure. Anaga had been the 'Superintendent of Wet Nurses' for Akbar when he was an infant, and she was very close to him. While Hamida and Humayun were in exile in Persia, she had played mother to the toddler. Now, she helped him escape from Biram Khan's control.

With the utmost secrecy, she arranged the 'hunting' expedition out of the Agra Fort. Her messengers were dispatched to have the Delhi Fort strengthened for Akbar's arrival. Once he reached Delhi, she sent out letters to all the senior Mughals that Akbar had broken away from Biram Khan.

What followed, shows up Biram Khan as a man of great character, while eighteen-year-old Akbar, unfortunately, handled the situation very clumsily. News of Akbar's breaking away initially shocked Biram Khan. He judged it was the work of Maham Anaga. Yet he decided to surrender immediately, leaving Agra for Delhi. In medieval India, if even sons approached their father's palace with a retinue of soldiers, they were suspected of plotting to overthrow their parent. Biram Khan's immediate surrender, along with his attendants, was considered suspicious by the harem. All might have ended happily between Akbar and the man he'd actually loved as a father, if Biram Khan's surrender had been accepted.

Instead, the women advising Akbar panicked. So Akbar sent word to Biram Khan to return to Agra and proceed on a pilgrimage to Mecca. Biram Khan immediately set out to obey this order, but then followed a series of vindictive moves by Maham Anaga, which ultimately proved too humiliating to the king's guardian, and he rebelled. Turning back from the journey to Mecca, Biram Khan decided to fight in order to clear his name.

He lost the battle but the old guardian was at last able to meet the young king again, though this time he was a prisoner. Face to face, the old affection between Biram Khan and Akbar resurfaced and Akbar treated his foster father with the utmost respect, pardoning him of all his supposed crimes. Having cleared his name, Biram Khan then chose to proceed to Mecca.

Sadly, in the deserts of Rajasthan, his group was ambushed by old rivals from Afghanistan. And the man who had saved the Mughal throne twice and laid the very foundation for the empire Akbar would eventually build, died because he had no one to defend him.

When news of Biram Khan's death reached the court, Akbar was filled with remorse. Luckily Biram Khan's family had survived. In a reversal of roles, nineteen-year-old Akbar chose to become the guardian of Biram Khan's four-year-old son, Abdur Rahim.

In the tug of war for power between Akbar's childhood protectors, his foster mother had won. But her victory was short-lived. Within months, her own son Adham Khan grew to become extremely arrogant and power hungry, repeatedly disobeying Akbar's orders. He was finally killed by Akbar himself, right outside the women's quarters, for having murdered Akbar's newly appointed prime minister. The shock and grief of her son's death at the hands of her foster son was too much for Maham Anaga. She died within a couple of months.

Biram Khan's son, Abdur Rahim, grew up to be every bit as talented as his father. He eventually rose to the highest official position in the kingdom, just as his father had.

Powerful petticoat governments

The reigns of two of the most powerful and enlightened Muslim rulers of the medieval period overlapped. The first ten years of Akbar's rule coincided with the last ten years of the greatest Turkish king, Suleiman the Magnificent.

The territory of this emperor of the Ottoman dynasty had stretched from Turkey's border into Europe. Hungary, most of the Balkans, West Asia and parts of North Africa were part of the Ottoman empire. Like his younger counterpart in Hindustan, this ruler too was immensely talented. He was considered one of the greatest Muslim poets, was an accomplished goldsmith and was called Suleiman the Lawmaker, because he updated the entire legal framework of his empire.

In the first decade of his rule, Akbar shakily settled into his throne, thanks to the immense support he received from the women of the house. Suleiman's last decade too witnessed a lot of the zenana's interference. His special fondness for a Russian slave whom he'd taken as his wife led to her inept and drunk son succeeding to the throne, and Suleiman's real heir was killed. Having set this precedence, the royal ladies began to play a bigger role in government throughout the following century.

10 Blood Feuds

Brothers killed and blinded brothers, and would execute or imprison their infant nephews to grab the throne—that was the Mughal world. There was no clear law about which son inherited the crown, so at the death of each monarch blood feuds began.

Akbar and his brother Mohammed Hakim too replayed Humayun's endless battles with his brothers. Dissatisfied with being just the governor of Kabul, Hakim had decided that he wanted a larger share of his big brother's growing empire. So he crossed the Indus river into Punjab.

Akbar rushed there. He was in a mood to settle blood feuds once and for all. But just as Babur's nemesis in Central Asia had been an Uzbeg warlord, Akbar too had to face a rebellion of Uzbegs in the years immediately after Biram Khan's death. Akbar quelled the rebellion once, and magnanimously pardoned the Uzbegs. They rebelled again, and then yet again, till Akbar ran out of patience and decimated them in battle.

At the same time, his Mirza cousins (with whom a running feud had begun in the days of Babur about who ought to rule over Kabul) rebelled. Each uprising that Akbar crushed seemed to spawn another. The *Akbar-nama* mentions over 140 rebellions. The Mirzas too met with defeat. An angry Akbar had the army's elephants trample the enemies.

Mohammed Hakim chose this moment to launch his campaign for more territory. Akbar moved to Punjab. But once he arrived there, the local support that Mohammed Hakim had been promised, vanished. The younger brother quickly retreated to Kabul, without exchanging any fire with his furious elder brother.

There was no comparison between the two brothers. Akbar had not lost a single battle for territory in years. Even in his twenties, his Indian empire had rapidly become the most powerful in the region. Mohammed Hakim himself was no threat to Akbar. But for other rebels in the empire, Hakim was a convenient figurehead. Even rebels geographically distant from Kabul would revolt against Akbar, declaring Hakim as their emperor. Over a span of fourteen years, a couple of great uprisings in Bengal and Bihar, nearly 1,000 miles away from Hakim's Kabul, were carried out supposedly in Hakim's name!

Obviously Hakim, whose talents and resources were limited, had no prior knowledge about these rebels' 'loyalty' towards him. But such revolts emboldened him. Both Hakim's entries into Punjab followed uprisings in Bengal. Maybe he believed that with Akbar's armies fighting on the eastern edge of his empire, the western boundaries would be difficult to protect. It's also possible that this relatively mild son of Humayun only wanted some more land. When his uncle Kamran had left Kabul and entered Punjab, Hakim's father Humayun generously granted the region to his younger brother, rather than fight him.

But Akbar was not generous where territory was concerned. When Hakim entered Punjab in 1580, Akbar planned to settle matters once and for all. He marched with 50,000 cavalrymen on a meticulously planned campaign. Once again, as Akbar approached, Hakim vanished, returning to Kabul. But Akbar followed him this time, driving his brother into the Afghan mountains. Though Hakim had ruled Kabul as a virtually independent ruler, he was technically merely its governor, under the Mughal court. So Akbar transferred the governorship to his sister, Bakhtunnisa Begum.

Hakim never again raised his head and his early death from palsy (induced by excessive drinking), prevented any further feuding between brothers.

Brother vs. brother and father vs. son

Life in Central Asia was so turbulent that a king of a small province was never sure he'd survive till his son reached his teens. Worse, even with many wives and hence many sons, not many children survived into adulthood. So for the Chugtai Timurids, there was no tradition of the eldest son becoming king. The fittest son became king, in a battle unto death, where he *proved* his fitness to rule.

This led to unimaginable bloodshed. We've seen poor Humayun, bound by a promise to his father Babur on his deathbed, not to fight his brothers. But that didn't buy him peace because his three brothers (not having

promised anything to father Babur on his deathbed) kept fighting him.

Akbar's tussle with Mohammed Hakim was mild by Mughal standards. Things got hotter in Jahangir's time. Apart from his tussle with son Khusrav, even before Akbar's death, his favourite son Khurram (Shah Jahan) broke out in rebellion, impatient to ascend the throne. After a series of battles that Shah Jahan lost, he begged his father for forgiveness and a tentative peace prevailed between father and son. But only because Jahangir held two of Shah Jahan's sons hostage!

But the battle of brothers that broke the Mughal empire was the one that took place following Shah Jahan's illness. There were four sons vying for the throne. Dara Shikoh, Shah Jahan's favourite and heir apparent, Shah Shuja, Aurangzeb and Murad.

In a protracted battle between the brothers that involved armies loyal to each of the four factions criss-crossing the country, Aurangzeb emerged the victor. After killing off his brothers, he was surprised to discover his father had recovered from his illness. Yet he certified him as unfit to rule and kept him under house arrest. Though Aurangzeb ruled over a long period of time, the wars of succession, along with his extended Deccan campaigns, turned the once-rich Mughal empire into a bankrupt state.

11 🐘 At Home in the Battlefield

In the scorching heat of an Agra summer, as the city struggled to go about its business, news arrived that Mughal troops in Malwa had been victorious. The palace erupted in celebration. For the king's household, it was a great day. This was Akbar's first attempt at expanding his kingdom after Biram Khan's banishment. A success in this campaign meant that Akbar was now an independent ruler. The twenty-year-old king had not gone to battle himself, but sent an army under the command of his foster brother Adham Khan, son of Maham Anaga.

Yet, while all of Agra celebrated, Akbar fumed. It was Mughal custom that victorious commanders turned over all their loot to the king, who then ceremoniously gifted back most of the treasure to the commander. Kings usually kept the best treasures. On Akbar's first victory without Biram Khan, Adham Khan had chosen not to send Akbar his due. Apart from a few elephants, Adham Khan kept most of the treasure, and certainly the best parts, for himself. Akbar would have none of this. He realized that Adham Khan needed to be dealt with immediately, before he rose to the stature of Biram Khan himself.

With lightning speed, Akbar left Agra. He moved fast, because he wanted to confront Adham Khan at Malwa, before his mother's messengers reached the scene of victory. In the height of the north Indian summer, Akbar dashed south, riding across 500 km, and caught Adham Khan completely by surprise. The army commander stood exposed, not having bothered to hide the loot from the conquest. A furious Akbar insisted on the royal portion of the treasure.

On another occasion, Akbar had returned to Fatepur Sikri after a victory in Gujarat. But on reaching home he learnt that his Mirza cousins whom he'd just defeated, had risen up in revolt all over again. Taking just a few thousand cavalrymen with him, Akbar dashed back across the Rajasthan desert and attacked the much larger army, defeating it yet again.

Akbar had enormous energy, was skilled in all forms of warfare and personal combat; and true to his Central Asian roots, was a nomad at heart. Like his ancestors Chenghis Khan and Timur the Lame, he was as comfortable on saddleback, as he was in a luxurious palace.

No battle was too tough for Akbar; and so he added more and more territory to his empire, which grew in all directions. From a boy–king who had leaned heavily on his foster father and foster mother, he stepped into the limelight on his own strength. By the time Akbar was in his thirties, he'd acquired a reputation for invincibility. Many potential enemies resisted going to war with him, because Akbar just never seemed to lose a battle!

Between 1565 and 1567, he quelled the rebellious Uzbeg chieftains within his empire. By a clever combination of marriage alliances, diplomatic treaties

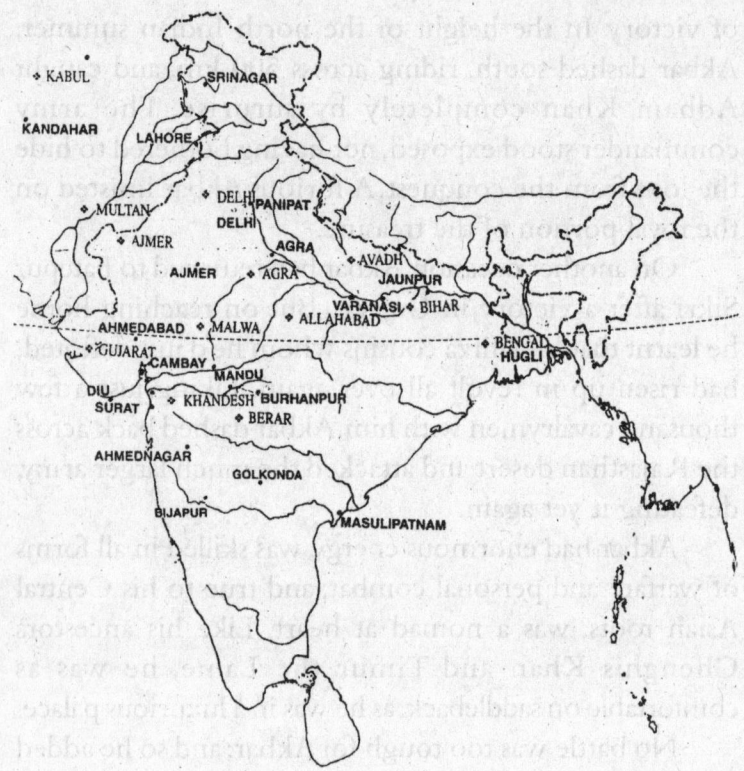

The Mughal empire in 1605

and fierce wars, most of Rajasthan was on his side. Gujarat became a Mughal province in 1573. Even the rebellious Bengal region was brought under control over the following years.

Once he had Kabul under him after Mohammed Hakim's defeat, Akbar went on to add other north-western provinces to the empire. Kashmir, Sind, Baluchistan, Makran and Kandahar all became Mughal territory, taking Akbar's borders right up to the Persian empire. By the time Akbar was in his fifties, Orissa, the famous Asisgarh fort and Ahmadnagar were also part of his empire.

Akbar was completely at home on the battlefield. Militarily he never faced a defeat. During a large part of his reign, across the vast Indian empire, peace prevailed except in one place . . . within the palace.

How to capture a fort
The Snake

A large 'snake' inched its way towards the walls of the Chittor Fort. It would take months to advance just a few feet. It was the famous 'sabat'. 5,000 men worked day and night, building it up with brick and mortar under heavy enemy fire. About a hundred died every day. This was the medieval way to storm into a fort.

Akbar spent six months in Rajasthan trying to break into the Chittor Fort. The surrounding areas were flat, and offered no protection for invading armies. So Akbar's only option was the 'sabat'. Bahadur Shah of Gujarat had stormed this fort earlier using this very technique. It involved building enormous corridors that originated beyond the range of the musketeers and archers defending the fort. The men who built it protected themselves with tough bull-hide shields, but still many died.

The sabat could accommodate about ten men walking abreast, and was even high enough for a man on an elephant. Its thick walls would protect anybody approaching the fort, and allowed invaders to dig deep into the fort walls to lay mines that exploded, breaching holes through which invading soldiers could enter.

Darkness gave both sides a chance to recover. The sabat builders worked with greater freedom, since they couldn't be shot at so easily by Rajput defenders. Those within the fort were able to block and repair any damage to the walls caused by Mughal cannons or exploding mines.

Chittor finally fell when, one night, Akbar's alert eye picked out someone he believed to be a leader overseeing repair operations within the fort. Taking aim, he fired and his bullet hit its target, killing Jai Mal, the general defending the fort. Though the Rajputs fought on valiantly till the end, Chittor was lost.

The Tower

But storming forts required a lot of time. A generation earlier, at Kalinjar, Sher Shah spent a year trying to capture the fort of Raja Kirat Singh of Bundelkhand. Though he used another technique very effectively, Sher Shah himself died of burns in the battle. Unlike the sabat that rose above the ground, Sher Shah built deep trenches towards the base of the fort. Besides that, close to the fort, he built a huge observation tower that slowly grew taller than the walls of the fort. From here Afghan snipers could aim and shoot at those within the fort. But in this case too, it took a year of round-the-clock, feverish building and thousands died, as the Rajputs bombarded the builders with arrows and gunfire. Kalinjar eventually fell to the Afghans, just before Sher Shah died.

The Purse

Just as there were long-drawn-out ways to breach a fort, defending forts was also a military art. Years later when Aurangzeb tried repeatedly to capture Golconda Fort from the Qutb Shahi dynasty, he was foiled by clever tactics. Before Aurangzeb's army arrived, Golconda forces had destroyed all buildings around the fort that could have been used as defences by the invading Mughals. All the tank walls were breached and water left to flow away and surrounding wells were poisoned. The defenders of Golconda were ensuring that life for the invading Mughal army was made miserable. Every tree, crop and plant was destroyed. This tactic worked. Aurangzeb's first attempt at capturing the fort failed even after spending 14 million rupees!

About six years later when another commander attempted and failed again, Aurangzeb himself tried. Months dragged on and the Mughal army was close to starvation; it looked like they would fail again. But the crafty emperor was able to bribe a commander of the Golconda army who opened the gates at night to let in the Mughal soldiers. So this impregnable fort finally fell due to a bribe.

12 🐘 A New City for Son Salim

'Ghosts!' screamed a voice, as women ran through the halls of the Agra palace, doors banging behind them. Children shrieked with terror. Those asleep tossed about restlessly, as nightmares disturbed them. The old women in the zenana clucked away with worry. This was not an auspicious sign.

Nothing good will come of this, they said, ominously. Somehow, the Agra palace did not seem welcoming to the Mughal women who'd migrated from Kabul and Lahore just a few years back, to make their home in Hindustan. When Akbar's teenaged queen, Ruqaiya Begum, lost her infant daughter, many in the palace felt it was the evil spirits at work.

Sure enough, by 1560, the sound of women weeping wafted through the gloomy palace corridors again. Just a month ago, the whole of Agra had celebrated the birth of Akbar's twin sons, Husain and Hasan. To the young eighteen-year-old king, it meant he had two heirs to his throne. But, within a few weeks, both infants died, plummeting the city into gloom. The future looked bleak. Akbar, not yet twenty, had already buried the first three children born to him.

For a Mughal king, life was very precarious. Most of Akbar's male ancestors hadn't lived past their thirties and forties. The reckless fighting, a nomadic life lived on the move, and bad habits like drinking and smoking opium sent many Mughal princes to an early grave.

Akbar's first marriage to his cousin Ruqaiya Begum happened when he was fifteen. He had married many times after that, but nine years later, none of his children were alive. Desperate, in 1562, the young king began making an annual pilgrimage to the tomb of Moinuddin Chisti, in Ajmer. He would set out barefoot and cover much of the 350 km from Agra on foot. He hoped that his prayers would fill his life with children.

He also began visiting the hermitage of another holy man, Salim Chisti, in Sikri, about 50 miles out of Agra. This saint reassured Akbar that he would eventually have three sons.

In 1569, when Akbar's Rajput wife, the daughter of Raja Bhara Mal, was expecting a child, the nervous king sent her to live in Sikri, under the protection of the revered saint. And that's where Akbar's first child to survive was born. Grateful, the king named his son after the saint, Salim.

By this time, Akbar had spent between five to eight years renovating the royal quarter of Agra. He added new palaces designed in the Gujarat and Bengal styles. He rebuilt the old fort of the Lodis in solid stone. In all he spent over three and a half million rupees—a fortune in those days—and it required a special tax to raise the funds.

But the rumours about the spirits began spreading beyond the household. Gradually, Akbar too got convinced that the place was unlucky for him. He would never be able to raise a happy family amongst ghosts. He decided to build his new capital in an auspicious place like Sikri. He would plan it himself. He would make sure that it was a place fit to raise the new prince. On Salim's birth, the country celebrated for a whole week. Prisoners were released and the poor fed. Raising a brand new city in the rocky hills of Sikri would take a few years, but just taking that decision seemed to turn Akbar's luck. Within three months a daughter was born to him. The following year, his second son Murad was born. And eventually Daniyal, his third son, arrived in 1572, followed by two daughters. Saint Salim Chisti's prophecy had come true.

A grateful king didn't give up his annual pilgrimage to the Ajmer shrine. Three months after Salim's birth, he walked the entire 350 km to Ajmer. He continued to visit the shrine, every year, till 1579.

The musician who cast a spell on an emperor
At Fatehpur Sikri there is a tank, called Anup Talao, with a small island in the middle. During cool evenings, warm summer nights or auspicious sunrises, musicians would set up their instruments by the tank and sing the raag appropriate for the hour. Akbar, who loved music, had designed it so that he could hear the musicians from his chambers. The women could also enjoy the music.

Indian folk tales are full of stories about Akbar's court, which had the famous Navratnas. The star amongst them was Tansen, the musician.

With Tansen, where truth ends and myth begins, it's difficult to tell. He was a fabulous vocalist and sitar player whose fame had spread across the country. He was born to a poor Brahmin, who had prayed to the Gwalior Sufi Pir, Mohammed Ghaus, for a child. When the boy was born, he was called Ramtanu and he showed a great talent for modulating his voice.

Legend has it that as a five year old, he frightened a band of musicians travelling through the forest by doing a perfect imitation of a tiger's growl. The leader of the group, Haridas, was very impressed and offered to train his voice. After some years spent as a pupil, Tansen went to the hermitage of Pir Mohammed Ghaus as his dying father had requested him to. There he learnt more about Persian and Central Asian music traditions. Gradually, by combining his training in the ancient Indian vocal traditions with the best of other music, Tansen became famous.

He moved from one royal patron to the other, till he reached the court of King Ramchandra of Rewa, in Central India. From there, on Akbar's request, he moved to the Mughal court.

One legend has it that jealous courtiers convinced Akbar to request the musician to sing Raag Deepak. This was rumoured to raise the temperature to such a level that unlit lamps would burst into flames. Tansen took up the challenge and the dark courtyard burst into light as the lamps came ablaze. The legend goes on to say that Tansen suffered a number of burns internally, while his burning skin was saved by his daughter who began singing Raag Megh Malhar, which brought rain.

Another tale suggests that Akbar's daughter Mehrunissa fell in love with Tansen and married him after being moved hearing him play the dilruba (an instrument like the sarangi).

Apart from the legends, Tansen left a very tangible musical legacy. He is credited with having brought order to the wide unstructured Indian classical music world. And it's his family and descendants that formed the Gwalior gharana, a musical tradition that continues today.

13 🐘 A City Lost to the Jungles

There was a constant roar of a hundred hammers pounding away on rock. The dust from the red sandstone being quarried was so thick that most workmen could barely recognize the men beside them. There was no time to exchange pleasantries at the building site at Sikri. Besides, one had to shout to be heard over the din of the stone mallets. Work was progressing at breakneck speed. The new prince Salim had been born. And Emperor Akbar wanted his city ready for the family to move into . . . fast.

Sometimes, through the haze of dust, workers sensed a presence—a fellow stonemason working as hard as them, lifting enormous, heavy slabs of red stone, walking effortlessly with it, not bowed down by his work. It was the discreet presence of guards that gave away the man's identity. It was Akbar himself!

Once he'd made up his mind to shift from Agra to Sikri, he moved heaven and earth to make it happen. He quarried with the masons; drew up plans himself with the best architects; with his passion for art, he personally supervised the decorations that embellished the buildings in Sikri. Every nook and corner of this new city that was growing out of the Aravalli hills had Akbar's signature on it.

When Babur came to India, he missed the cool mountains of Fergana very much. He laid out formal gardens in the Persian style wherever he stopped in memory of the places he grew up in, but had left behind. The gypsy king Humayun didn't spend enough time in India to leave his architectural stamp on the country, but his widow built Humayun's mausoleum in the classical Persian style.

Akbar was different. To him, India was home. It was in a remote Rajput fortress that he was born. His Rajput wife had borne him his first son. His closest associates and leading members of his administration were Rajputs and Hindus from other states. He was the first Mughal with deep cultural roots in Hindustan. No city built by him would copy the classical Persian style. Sikri would reflect Akbar's very own style.

He used local building materials, building techniques and architectural features, with just an element of West Asia. Instead of the signature arches of Islamic structures, royal buildings in Sikri used the Hindu method of pillar, beam and bracket. Instead of marble, Akbar used red sandstone to very dramatic effect. While Persians decorated brick and masonry structures with mosaic tiles, Akbar used marble merely to inlay the red stone. The palaces of Sikri, with their chhatris, seem like Hindu structures. Yet their open layout is West Asian.

In the midst of planning and building, Akbar had other kingly duties like conquering new territories or stamping out rebellions. In June 1573, Akbar returned to the growing city after defeating the king of Gujarat,

Muzaffar Shah, and putting down an uprising of his cousins, the Mirzas. Entering Sikri after these two victories, he felt he ought to rename the emerging city Fatehpur (City of Victory) Sikri. And at the entrance of the grand Jama Musjid being built, Akbar ordered a new gateway to be erected. The eighteen-storey-high Bulund Darwaza was Akbar's dramatic statement of how he, still in his thirties, viewed himself: as a king following a path of his own making.

Fatehpur Sikri was a beautiful city, and true, it seemed to bring the young king good luck. It was here that his children were born. It was in these rugged hills that Akbar began his personal search for a religion that answered all his doubts. It was in this city that Akbar's famous night-long religious debates began. He had a special Idabat Khana (House of Religion) built. Here gurus, saints and experts of all religions gathered to exchange views.

But Fatehpur Sikri also had a terrible water problem. The well water was brackish so Akbar had embankments built around a lake close by for the city's needs. Delhi and Agra had extreme climates, but at Fatehpur Sikri the summers were hotter and the winters even colder than at the older capital cities.

Once, when the royal family was picnicking beside the lake, the dam burst. Luckily no one from Akbar's group was harmed. But parts of the city got flooded and many others lost their lives. The lake's embankments had to be rebuilt.

Eventually, Akbar was forced to abandon the city. Not because of the water or the weather, but for one, his Indian territories had become too vast to administer from one capital city. He saw trouble brewing in the north-west borders and felt being in Lahore gave him a better chance to protect the country and conquer new territory. Secondly, Akbar was descended from the nomadic tribes of Central Asia. Fourteen years was as long as he could remain in one place before he got the urge to move on.

By 1585, Akbar moved to Punjab. The reason he'd originally come to Sikri was for Sheikh Salim Chisti's company and blessings. The saint had long since died. Akbar returned to this city only once more in his life, in 1601, while returning from a military campaign in the Deccan. By that time the jungle had re-conquered the city. Only the royal quarter remained, like a ghost town, loyally preserved by Saint Salim Chisti's family.

Akbar and the Portuguese—a mystery

In 1573, a young Akbar was in Gujarat, putting down a fierce rebellion by his cousins, the Mirzas. One version of history reports that he found out the Portuguese, who virtually controlled the sea routes in the Indian Ocean, were supporting the Mirzas, so he opened up negotiations with the foreigners.

Portuguese memoirs of the time however claim that Akbar's subsequent victory over the Mirzas was because of Portuguese diplomacy. Akbar's historian Abul Fazl claims the opposite. Either way, Akbar invited the foreigners to his court to open an embassy at Fatehpur Sikri.

Winning Gujarat and the rich city of Surat meant that those in Akbar's empire now had direct access to a port on the way to Mecca and Medina. Surat was a busy port and Akbar's revenue from Gujarat became immense. Yet, a few miles out of the port, Akbar's ships were at the mercy of the Portuguese. Then why does the *Akbar-nama* report that there was the best of relationships between Akbar and the Portuguese?

There were three important Portuguese missions to Akbar's court. The first arrived in 1573, with Akbar eager to learn about the science, art and religion of the foreigners. And they were eager to convert the king! Akbar seems to have enjoyed widening his knowledge of Europe and Christianity, but had no intentions of converting himself. He did hand over ten-year-old Murad to the priests to be taught Christianity, though. The Portuguese participated in discussions at the Ibadat Khana, but that was as far as it went.

In 1580, the second mission arrived, this time with a priest from an aristocratic Italian family, Rudolph Aquaviva. Again, any hopes of converting the king and hence turning India into a domain under the Roman Catholic Pope were dashed. Akbar treated the Portuguese well, housing them in the royal quarters, and became good friends with Aquaviva. A third mission, this time headed by the grand nephew of St. Francis Xavier himself, arrived in Akbar's court in Lahore in 1595. They were allowed to convert people, build churches and open hospitals, but the mission's prime focus of converting the king failed.

While polite diplomacy and religious discussions were on at court, on the west coast of India Portuguese power was increasing. Portuguese pirates raided Indian ships travelling to West Asia. Trade between Surat and ports in the south, like Calicut, was again controlled by Portuguese ships. One really wonders why Akbar did not build up a strong Indian navy. He, of all kings, saw their power grow during the period of his reign. Under his watch, the land route to Persia through Kabul and Kandahar was virtually abandoned. Though the sea was infested with pirates, it was still safer and faster than travelling through what is now Afghanistan. How could Akbar, a man of such vision, have failed to realize that the future lay with the ones who controlled the seas?

14 🐘 Suspended Saints!

The new young guard on duty on the ramparts of the fort shivered in the night. He drew his blanket more tightly around him as the cold December wind whipped against his face, making his eyes water. He longed to curl up in a sheltered nook of the fort and catch a few hours of sleep. But he shook himself awake. He thought he'd heard something.

Suddenly alert, he looked down the line of the fort to see if the other guards on duty had noticed the sound. It seemed to be coming from somewhere below him— a sort of creaking of wooden planks and rustling of rope. Worse still, the sound was getting louder . . . whatever it was, seemed to be coming closer!

In a panic, the guard ran towards a bastion in the fort to get a clearer view of the steep naked walls that plunged hundreds of feet down into the darkness. Then he saw it: a charpoy with what looked like a dead body wrapped and tied on to it was being slowly drawn up the walls by ropes that disappeared into one of the balconies projecting out of the fort wall.

What was *happening*? Had somebody been murdered and was his body being hidden? Or was this a dreadful attempt to smuggle a thief into the palace? The poor guard was too new on the job to make sense of what he'd just seen. He ran as fast as he could to the head guard on duty. Breathlessly he reported what he'd seen, expecting everybody in the guardroom to erupt into quick action. But the older guards just laughed at him.

That night the youngster learnt about the strange ways of the emperor Akbar. That blanket-wrapped 'body' was no thief, but the Sufi saint Sheikh Tajudin. And no, he was not being punished for some crime. It was Akbar's habit to have night-long discussions with learned men of different religions. He'd devised this method which offered him total privacy. The saint would be hauled up the fort walls strapped to his charpoy, which would hang suspended just outside the window of Akbar's bedroom, and through the window, the young emperor and the saint would talk through the night!

There were others too, who had stayed awake answering the restless Akbar's innumerable questions. A respected Hindu saint called Debi spent many a night suspended in midair outside Akbar's window, discussing topics like the transmigration of souls. Mohammed Yazdi, a Sunni mullah who later turned against Akbar, had also been hauled up and suspended many a night.

Abul Fazl, Akbar's friend, courtier and official biographer reports that the king had unlimited energy and slept barely a few hours every night. His night-long discussions with saints in no way affected his day's routine.

The influences in Akbar's childhood were varied. Though the Timurid family of Central Asia were Sunni Muslims, they were not religious. Culture, science, natural history and technology were more important to Babur and his descendants. Besides this, Biram Khan, who played a father's role after Humayun's death, was a Shia Muslim. Of the many unsuccessful tutors Akbar had as a child, there was one who exposed him to Sufism. Then in his palace, he attended the pujas performed by his Rajput Hindu wife, the princess of Ambar and mother of his eldest son, Salim. Akbar saw that each religion answered some of his doubts, but no one religion had all the answers for him.

In Fatehpur Sikri Akbar set up the Ibadat Khana, or the house of worship, in 1575. Initially, Muslims of all sects met here to debate. Then in 1578, the night-long discussions were thrown open to experts of all religions. Jains, Buddhists, Hindus, Parsis, Jews and Christians were all welcomed. When these sessions became too heated or argumentative, Akbar must have retired to his bedroom for a quieter 'window discussion'.

After Akbar had invited the religious head of the Parsi community, Dastur Mahyarji Rana to the palace, a sacred fire was set up in the palace. Akbar's later deep friendship with Birbal influenced him further in the matter of Sun worship. Birbal was supposed to have convinced Akbar that since humanity received light and sustenance from the sun, the sun deserved the highest reverence. When the Jain sage, Hiravijaya Suri, walked to Fatehpur Sikri from Gujarat on Akbar's invitation, Akbar turned virtually vegetarian. He even gave up hunting and fishing, and released caged birds and animals.

Akbar's personal lifestyle soon incorporated what he considered the best aspects from every religion. Thrice he invited the Portuguese of Goa to set up missions in the Mughal territory. One son, Murad, was sent to the Portuguese Christian mission in Lahore to learn all about Christianity. Another son, Daniyal, was sent to Raja Bhara Mal's home to be brought up by his wife in a Hindu Rajput household.

Akbar assigned various Hindu texts to be translated into Persian. The Vedas, Upanishads and the Mahabharata were all soon available to be read in Persian. Right through Akbar's life he was constantly searching for a more complete understanding of God. And though he personally remained a Muslim, he encouraged Indians to choose whichever religion they wanted to practise. When compared to Europe of that period, Indians enjoyed unheard-of religious freedom.

Eventually Akbar lost interest in the Ibadat Khana. He himself stopped attending it and by 1582, it ceased to exist. It was not that Akbar lost interest in religion. It was just that he realized that most so-called religious 'experts' couldn't address his queries. He needed to find his own answers.

Though the multi-religion discussions petered off, Akbar's court continued to represent the multi-cultural nature of the country he ruled. His most trusted ministers and commanders were Hindus. Raja Todar Mal, a Rajput, was given complete freedom as revenue minister of the empire. Raja Bhagwan Das and his adopted son, Raja Man Singh were generals that Akbar had implicit faith in. And one of his closest friends was a poor Brahmin called Mahesh Das, who'd been brought to the Mughal court by Raja Bhagwan Das. All Mahesh Das had to recommend him was a sense of humour and a flair for poetry. Yet, though he was fourteen years older than Akbar, they became the closest of friends. Akbar's love for this palace wit elevated him to the rank of a Raja—Raja Birbal.

As Akbar grew older, he realized as only a true visionary could, that his vast and multi-religious empire needed something common to bind it. While he was alive, his extraordinarily strong persona was the glue that held together the largest empire in the world. But Hindustan was a country divided by a thousand languages. Dozens of religions were practised freely within its borders. And within religions were castes, sub-castes and other differentiators. Akbar probably dreaded the divisive religious forces that would tear apart his beloved country when he passed on.

He formulated a doctrine of his own for living an honest and harmonious life, deliberately rejecting all that he didn't believe in from the various religions, including his own. Stirring together all that was good from every creed, he drew up plans for a new way of living—Din-i-Ilahi. He went to great pains to point out that nobody needed to give up their religion to follow the path of Din-i-Ilahi. All they needed to shed was their centuries-old distrust of other faiths. Din-i-Ilahi was meant to be a common code that would bind Indians of different religions.

Freedom of worship: Europe vs. Hindustan

Under Akbar's rule, all Indians were allowed to follow any faith they chose, and to convert to any religion they wanted. For over 500 years before him, parts of India that fell to Muslim rule had faced different kinds of religious persecution, from mild to severe. Early in his reign, Akbar first abolished the pilgrim tax, then the jizya, the tax for non-Muslims. From there, he went on to pass laws that took into account the diverse nature of his empire. Cow slaughter was prohibited in accordance with Hindu custom. There were Hindu customs that he disapproved of. Child marriage was one, which he tried to prevent by ordering marriages to be registered. He disapproved of Sati, but instead of banning it entirely, ruled that very young widows were to be prevented from performing this sacrifice. This king, who loved blood sports as a youngster, gave up hunting after his close association with Jain priests. The holy books of all religions were translated into different languages.

In Europe, on the other hand, the notorious Inquisition had been set up. This religious court that existed in a mild form in Italy took on a very fundamentalist and cruel approach in Spain and Portugal. Spain had been ruled by Muslim kings for centuries, starting from the 8th century. By Akbar's time, Roman Catholic kings had re-conquered almost all of Spain. They set out to stamp out all signs of West Asian Muslims and Jews from their country. Thousands of Muslims and Jews converted to Christianity just to save their lives; even more fled the continent. While the Pope in Rome sought protection

for these converts, the Spanish kings persecuted even those who'd converted.

A mere rumour about a convert secretly practising his old religion could result in him being burnt alive. Thousands died, burning at the stake, with almost no genuine evidence against them. By contrast, in Akbar's India, the king himself sat up all night debating the pros and cons of each religion with Hindu, Muslim, Jain, Portuguese Catholic and Parsi priests!

One spot of Christian fundamentalism did exist in India—at Goa. Here, in a tiny pocket of land right at Akbar's doorstep, a Portuguese Viceroy ruled over a small state where Hindus were brutally persecuted and mass conversions took place. Ironically, Rudolph Aquaviva, who'd just spent three years living in the royal quarters at Akbar's invitation in a haven of religious freedom, returned to Goa and died, a victim of his own people's religious intolerance. Walking past a village where the Portuguese had desecrated the temple and wilfully slaughtered a cow, Aquaviva and three other priests died in the Hindu riot that followed.

15 🐘 Polo-playing Princesses and Crack-shot Queens

Once, when Prince Salim was out on a hunt with one of his favourite wives, the Rajput princess Jagat Gosain, the couple was suddenly attacked by a lion. As a youngster, under father Akbar's sharp eye, Salim had proved to be talented in every field. He was a good student, a keen lover of art and music, fearless in battle and an excellent shot. But his discovery of alcohol in his early teens ruined him. Constant drinking and smoking opium dulled the prince's sharp reflexes. And while he'd once been a crack-shot, now his hands shook.

On that fateful day, Jagat Gosain rose to the occasion. She grabbed a rifle and shot the lion dead, saving the life of Akbar's heir. That episode was typical of the role played by the royal women during Mughal times—tough and smart enough to take matters into their hands when the men failed.

The nomadic life of the early Mughals ensured the women were as hardy as the men. When the teenaged Babur's father died in a building collapse, his grandmother Aisan Daulat took him under her wing. While Babur's innumerable uncles and cousins jostled for the kingdom of Fergana, the wise old lady, who lived camped out in the open Central Asian steppes, ensured Babur sat on the throne.

As his fortunes shifted—winning a city one day, only to lose it a month later—his mother, Qutlaq Nigar, kept him company. She travelled with him through hostile territory on all his military campaigns.

When Akbar built his new capital at Sikri, a section of it was cordoned off as a school for the young girls of the royal family. All Mughals believed deeply in education. Princesses were taught mathematics, astronomy, sciences, the Koran, and the classics from Persian and Turki, and a whole lot more. Female tutors, whom the young princesses affectionately called Atun Mama, were selected from very scholarly families. The tutor of Shah Jahan's daughter, Jahanara, was Sati-ul-nisa, the sister of the court poet.

With such academic backing, it's not surprising that Gulbadan Begum was able to write her brother Humayun's biography with ease. Salima Begum was Akbar's very talented cousin who'd married Biram Khan after the Mughals reclaimed India. When he died, Akbar married her and adopted her son. She was a well-known poet, who wrote under the pen name Makhfi (the concealed one). Poets in purdah seemed to be a common Mughal tradition. Four generations later, Aurangzeb's talented daughter, Zebunnisa, also wrote poetry under the name 'The Concealed One'.

Nur Jahan, Jahangir's favourite wife, wrote poetry. Akbar's great granddaughter, Jahanara, wrote a famous biography of Akbar's favourite saint, Khwaja Moinnudin Chisti of Ajmer. Many of these clever women collected books, maintained good libraries and supported calligraphers and artists. In the days before the printing press came to India, calligraphy was a very important and admired art.

Having enjoyed the benefit of education themselves, many royal women tried to educate less fortunate women. Princesses were given very generous allowances from the royal treasury. Akbar's aunts, his mother, his cousins, daughters and granddaughters spent hefty amounts of their allowances building mosques with madrassas attached. So though the royal women lived in purdah, and were never seen by commoners, their influence was felt far beyond the zenana.

Apart from all these intellectual pursuits, the women obviously learnt riding because they were known to play polo! Many of them enjoyed hunting. Nur Jahan was a keen shot and was famous for once killing four tigers in six shots!

With their allowances, some enterprising royal women owned ships and financed trade and pilgrim expeditions from the ports of Gujarat, thus investing their money the way present-day women do—buying shares in companies!

Of course, Mughal women also spent unbelievable sums on their wardrobe and on jewellery. But they were known for their charity too. Nur Jahan was very generous, with a soft spot for orphans. She arranged the marriage of hundreds of such girls.

Humayun had brought to India the tradition of weekly fairs of the nomadic Central Asian tribes in which men and women participated. But the Indian version had a twist. It was run only by women from royal and noble families and was open only to noblemen and the king. It was called the Meena Bazaar and was held on important festivals. The women could command any price for the luxury goods they sold, recklessly bargaining with the king himself. The huge profits made from these sales were given to charity.

But the most important role played by the royal Mughal women was in matters of state. The uzuk or the royal ring used to stamp important documents was kept by the first lady of the empire. In Akbar's case, it was with his mother, Hamida Banu. So the women got to read the most important documents of the empire before putting the emperor's seal on it. Also, important meetings with ministers were held in the Hall of Private Audience (the Diwan-i-Khaas), with the leading ladies of the family in attendance but unseen behind a screen! Once when Jahangir was considering sentencing a nobleman closely linked to the royal family through marriage to death for treason, Akbar's wife Salima Begum called him from behind the screen to hear the women's opinion. They wanted mercy to be shown to this traitor and Jahangir listened to them and spared the man's life. When military might failed; when the best statesmen in the land gave up, the women stepped in. They were particularly successful in bringing about peace when brothers fought brothers and sons rose in rebellion against their father, the king.

Everything Akbar had built up over four decades

would have been ruined in the tussle between him and his son, Salim, if the women had not stepped out and taken control.

Going to battle against a queen

Deep in the forests of present-day Madhya Pradesh, a queen was doing what many kings were famous for—shifting her capital. Chauragarh was the capital of one of five independent Gond kingdoms. The region was heavily forested and filled with rocky hills and steep ravines. Yet Rani Durgavati, queen of the Gond state of Gadha (or Garha), felt Singaurgarh, which had a very strategically located fort, would make a better capital.

She was a smart queen. She came from the Chandela dynasty. When her husband Dalpathshah died, her son Vir Narayan was only five years old. She decided to rule as the regent and made a great success of it. The people of thousands of villages in her kingdom lived in prosperity.

Naturally, the wealth of her kingdom attracted her neighbours. Baz Bahadur, the ruler of neighbouring Malwa, decided that the Gond riches could be his, since all he needed to do was defeat a 'mere' queen.

Durgavati went out to meet Baz Bahadur in battle and defeated him thoroughly. Peace now reigned on her western border . . . but only for a short time. Akbar's army soon moved into the region. After Mughal general Asaf Majid Khan defeated Baz Bahadur and took over the country, the wealth of Rani Durgavati's kingdom seemed very tempting. Earlier, Mughal emissaries had been sent to the Rani, suggesting she become a subject

state to the Mughal emperor, like many of the Rajput kingdoms. The Rani had refused.

So from Singaurgarh, the Rani planned for a battle to the finish. Asaf Khan, with Akbar's permission, moved into the Gond kingdom. The Rani, knowing she was outnumbered and outgunned, chose to fight from the Narrai valley, which was surrounded by two rivers and a hillside. The way this smart queen set the stage for a battle between her tiny army and the mighty Mughals seems very much like how Babur planned the Battle of Panipat against a phenomenally bigger army. Like Babur, Rani Durgavati's strategy paid off. She won the battle, trouncing the general and chasing him out of the region.

With the advantage on her side, and her army's superior knowledge of the terrain, the Rani wanted to pursue the Mughals through the night. But, unfortunately, all her generals refused. This proved to be fatal for the Gonds. Asaf Khan used the night to get heavy artillery into the region and was prepared for battle the next day.

The Rani and her eighteen-year-old son led the army into battle. Against all odds, the Gonds fought on tenaciously, winning the early rounds, but on 24 June 1564, the queen got wounded, and rather than face capture or allow the enemy to kill her, she stabbed herself with her dagger.

Her son Vir Narayan fought on, finally taking refuge in the fort at Chauragarh that his mother had earlier abandoned as being not safe enough. The queen had been right. The Mughal army was able to capture and kill Vir Singh at Chauragarh Fort with ease.

16 🐘 The Graffiti Artist

The emperor's elephant lumbered through the streets of Fatehpur Sikri. As usual, there were other elephants ahead, with mounted horsemen and foot soldiers making up the procession. Way back in 1564, when Akbar was just twenty-two, there had been a near fatal attempt to kill the king. A slave, obviously on the orders of someone more powerful, had shot at Akbar from the balcony of a seminary, when he was returning from a shrine in Delhi. The arrow pierced deeply into Akbar's right shoulder, but fortunately caused no serious harm. The slave was immediately killed, yet no one learned which powerful nobleman was behind the plot. So apart from the tight security, it was just another normal day in Akbar's hectic schedule . . . till the young king's sharp eye spotted something. He immediately called out for his elephant to be stopped.

The security men in the procession froze. Had Akbar noticed a potential danger that they had missed? Without saying why, Akbar asked for the procession to change direction. He'd seen something that had excited him immensely and he led his entourage towards it.

On the walls of a building off the main thoroughfare Akbar had seen beautiful drawings! He couldn't believe his eyes and just *had* to have a second look. Some unknown artist had filled the wall spaces with what seemed like a magic hand. His eager scouts soon ran about finding more and more walls covered with drawings by this mysterious artist. Akbar would not rest till he found out who the artist was. How had such talent been allowed to escape his notice?

Akbar's love for drawing and art dated back to his childhood. Art class was the only one he did not bunk! He himself was a very talented artist and continued taking art classes even as a busy emperor. Whatever the demands of ruling over a vast and growing empire, Akbar tried his best to keep his appointment with art teacher Khwaja Abdus Samad.

Akbar's love of art was so famous that artists from all over Hindustan, Iran and the Central Asian kingdoms flocked to the court of this powerful and generous king. In Akbar's art studios or karkhanas, hundreds of artists worked for a generous salary. Eighteen of them were acknowledged master painters whose names appeared in the margins of the famous Mughal miniature paintings of that time.

Akbar was puzzled. When the whole of the East knew that his studio's doors were open to artists, why had this mysterious person chosen to waste his talents on the walls of alleyways? Soon the mystery was solved. Akbar's scouts had traced the artist and brought him before the king. The emperor's heart melted. Standing before him was a young boy who looked petrified. His ragged appearance obviously meant he was miserably poor. He looked as though he was expecting to get thrashed for scribbling on the walls. Akbar discovered that the boy, Daswanth's father, was a poor palanquin bearer.

Overnight the royal art teacher, Khwaja Abdus Samad, acquired a second student—the boy from the streets. From using charcoal and mud paste, Daswanth now had art materials worth a fortune. Lapis lazuli stone mined from Badakshan was ground into a powder to make blue paint and red ochre from the mineral geru. Vegetable dyes like indigo, the fruit hironji and other carefully prepared mixtures were his to use as he pleased. For ten years Daswanth lived in Akbar's karkhana. Within just a few months of training, carefully supervised by Akbar, Daswanth surpassed his teacher. Unfortunately, the boy was prone to depression. He barely enjoyed a decade of fame, before he committed suicide.

Artists working together in Akbar's studios were in the process of creating a revolution in art. Years ago, when Humayun had been in exile in Persia, he convinced two well-known painters to return with him to Kabul. These two men, trained in the Safavid or Iranian miniature style, set up the Mughal art department. They were guided partly by Islamic traditions that prohibited portraits and figures of animals. Safavid art was closely linked to the illustration of Persian classics. So to really appreciate early Mughal miniatures, a viewer needed to know the Persian stories behind them.

Akbar broke with this tradition. Of his eighteen master artists, thirteen were Hindus. He encouraged artistic ideas from all countries to bloom. From his time onwards, miniatures began to record court life with recognizable images of the emperor and his courtiers. Animals and nature were depicted in great detail. With Akbar's love for manuscripts, artists worked constantly on providing illustrations for those books.

The Department of Translation

The work of the karkhana was tightly linked to Akbar's Department of Translations. These two, in turn, were linked to the army of calligraphers, paper makers and book binders that Akbar employed. Even though the printing press had been invented in Europe by Akbar's time and many European ambassadors and traders had gifted him printed books, Akbar gave them away. To him the manuscript was the ultimate treasure—it brought together the artistry of an individual calligraphist, the illustrations of numerous master painters, and the craft of the book binder.

Though Akbar himself never learnt to read and write, he was brilliant and educated! He loved books. His thirst for knowledge was unquenchable, and he was prepared to look for answers in any language.

The translation department had scholars translating Greek texts to Persian and Sanskrit; Sanskrit books on mathematics to Persian and Turki; the classics of all languages were made more accessible to scholars; and with Akbar's interest in the Christian faith, even Portuguese translators worked for him. Within the close network of nobles, Akbar had phenomenal talent to choose from. His biographer and close friend, Abul Fazl (the author of the *Ain i Akbari*)

and his brother, Abul Faiz, were responsible for this department and had themselves translated a number of books.

Akbar's adopted son, Abdur Rahim, who also happened to be the top official of the empire—the Khan-i-khannan—was a linguist. He wrote in Arabic, Persian, Sanskrit and Turki. Somewhere in his hectic schedule he found the time to translate Babur's autobiography, *Babur-nama*, from Turki to Persian.

Akbar also requested his beloved aunt, Gulbadan Begum, to write her personal accounts of Babur and Humayun's reigns. He also asked Humayun's loyal aide, Jauhar, to write his memoirs. Both these books were to be the reference for Abul Fazl as he wrote Akbar's biography. Badauni, a court chronicler who later became a critic of Akbar's, was assigned to translate the Mahabharata. And as the writing went on, artists worked on illustrating these works.

At the time of Akbar's death, his library had over 24,000 entirely handcrafted manuscripts, worth millions of rupees.

17 🐘 The Mystery of the Prince Who Vanished

Akbar's campaign against the Raja of Mewar, one of the rare Rajputs who refused to ally with the Mughal court, began in 1566, and would drag on for decades, finally ending only in 1615, a decade after Akbar's death. On one such march in 1576, when the Mughal soldiers close to the royally caparisoned elephant looked up to their 'commander', they saw a seven-year-old boy! Prince Salim, later to become Jahangir, had been given the command of 10,000 soldiers during the long-drawn-out Mewar campaign. That was the Mughal way. Of course, the prince was under the watchful eye of his guardian, the Khan-i-khannan, Abdur Rahim.

Each generation of this family of Chugtai Tartars had seen turbulent times. Babur's father had died when he was a young teenager. Akbar himself was crowned king at thirteen. These princes were born to rule and there was no time to waste in childhood. They had to be exposed to the horrors and dynamics of war at the earliest.

As a twelve year old, Prince Salim, still the apple of his father's eye and the pet of the zenana ladies, accompanied Akbar on his Kabul mission. It was to settle matters with Akbar's younger brother Muhammed

89

Hakim. Fearless, a good marksman, swordsman and leader of men, Salim was given a large command. Then, having proved himself on the battlefield, he was given charge of two departments—justice and festivities—to get a taste of administration. This too was under the guidance of the able administrator, Adbur Rahim.

Yet, it seems in this case the Mughal tradition of preparing a prince for his father's early death had backfired. Akbar was the first among the Mughals to establish peace, prosperity and stability within his empire. Besides his immense power over a vast land, he was also in the best of health. So here was a prince, trained from infancy to rule, finding nothing to rule. Raring to go, eager for adventure, action and prepared to take any risk, by all accounts Salim was immensely talented. Yet for some reason, his father was reluctant to give Salim a province to rule. All Salim's excellent training could not be put to use.

Akbar's fatal delay in engaging his sons in ruling Hindustan when they were ready cost him his children. One by one he lost them to alcohol and opium. A trained commander of men when he was just twelve, Salim suddenly had to wait in the sidelines as his father refused to give him any independent command.

He soon took to the bottle and to opium. By his early twenties, he was an addict. Akbar, who did not enjoy wine as much as his father Humayun or his grandfather Babur had, could not understand his son's weakness. As Salim's waywardness increased, Akbar began to favour him less. His limited responsibilities were removed. With less work to occupy the prince, he now spent more time drinking.

It seems that the moment his sons became old enough to rule, Akbar considered them as competitors and shifted his affection and attention to his grandsons. Prince Salim, for whose birth Akbar had walked barefoot to Ajmer; whose circumcision, first introduction to the alphabet, and first exposure to battle were all state occasions recorded in great detail by royal scribes, suddenly vanished from the official Mughal chronicles after the Kabul campaign. What could this twelve-year-old prince have done to earn his father's displeasure? Or did the fault lie with the father?

Only in 1591 does Prince Salim resurface in Mughal chronicles, that too for just a brief moment, when shadowy references are made to Salim in relation to an attempt to assassinate Akbar. This was never proved, and after that the prince vanishes from the books again!

Dressing for battle Mughal style

Mughal soldiers did not wear a uniform, so the spectacle of them marching dressed in various flashing colours was fabulous. The cavalry was the cream of the army. Soldiers were handpicked, and most important, the horses they rode were of the best Arabian stock. They were imported all the way from Turkey, Iraq and Persia.

Both rider and horse were covered in chain mail (metal, chain-linked, flexible armour). Each soldier carried

a sword, a two-yard long lance, a bow and a quiver of arrows, a shield and had a gun strapped on to his back. Helmets with ear-guards along with eye-catching gems encrusted all over added to a soldier's dashing look. Yak-tail tassels fluttered from the edges of the embroidered and gem-encrusted saddles.

Mughal noblemen really dressed up for war. Raja Todar Mal, Akbar's revenue minister and a very astute commander of armies, even went so far as to have his prize horses' hooves shod in gold horseshoes!

Elephants too were decked out for war. A close look at any print of a Mughal miniature featuring a war scene will tell you that dressing up the elephants was equally important—with bells around their necks, chains draped under their tails, anklets on their feet, forehead ornaments and rich fabric draped over their backs. A well-dressed elephant reflected the prestige of the emperor.

18   The Battle Against the Bottle

It was 1591, and forty-nine-year-old Akbar lay on his deathbed. Dark rumours buzzed through the palace about it being a possible case of poisoning. The king, whose health had been in excellent condition, had suddenly fallen ill with a stomach ailment. The best physicians were summoned to treat him but no medicine seemed to work.

On whom would the blame fall? Protecting the emperor from poison involved an elaborate routine of checks and counter checks. To begin with, except for royal banquets, Akbar ate alone in the harem. Getting the food to the harem was a military operation in itself. Specialist cooks, who each were required to cook only that one dish that they were expert in, tucked in their sleeves and covered their mouths and noses so that their breath would not contaminate the royal food. They presented their preparations to the taster or Bakawal. If he approved, it was passed to the head taster or Mir Bakawal to taste the food again. When he was satisfied, the preparation was placed in the appropriate dish, covered, wrapped in rich cloth and the flaps and folds of the cloth were sealed and imprinted by the Bakawal's stamp. The name and number of each dish that was sealed was then written down on a sheet of paper, to be counter checked before the emperor ate. That way, no extra untasted dish could find its way on to the emperor's plate.

Since dozens of dishes were prepared for every meal, a long train of bearers had to carry the food. They were escorted by armed guards into the harem, so that nobody could exchange a dish or approach the bearers.

The emperor ate only from dishes whose seals were broken in front of him. The food was then tasted again in the presence of the emperor and with the Mir Bakawal in attendance. Poisoning Akbar under such elaborate supervision seemed virtually impossible. So was it a harem plot? Or was it the work of the young, restless Prince Salim, who everybody now knew was not on good terms with his father?

Rumours flew thick when a delirious Akbar was heard to murmur in his semi-conscious state, 'Baba Shaikhuji' his affectionate pet name for his eldest son 'Since all this sultanate will devolve on thee, why hast thou made this attack on me?'

Akbar eventually pulled through this crisis. Though Salim's role in the episode was never proven, Akbar's affection shifted to his younger son Murad. But it was too late. Murad's alcoholism was far advanced and no amount of treatment or delayed parental attention could save him. When the prince who was second in line for the throne was just twenty-nine years old, he died. That was Akbar's first taste of defeat. He, who had never lost a single battle for territory and was able to protect the distant boundaries of the largest empire in the world of that time, had lost his first battle . . . within the walls of his home. And he lost it to an enemy he had no skills to combat—alcohol.

Murad's death from drink led to Akbar panicking. His hopes then shifted to Daniyal. But this third son too was a physical and psychological wreck. Akbar tried every trick he could to keep him from drinking. He threatened his son's drinking buddies with imprisonment if they procured wine for Daniyal. Guards were posted at Daniyal's residence to check those going in. But Daniyal's friends proved too smart. Through bribery and clever camouflage they were able to keep their drunken friend happy with a steady supply. Eventually, by the time Daniyal was thirty-one, he too would die from drink.

But before that, his father's temporary favour served to make matters worse. Prince Salim was not going to give up without a fight. However much others feared his father, Salim was fearless.

The Wine of Nishapour

In 1988, for the first time in over 900 years, a renowned Persian scholar from Iran—Karim Emami—translated the famous Persian poems of Omar Khayyam into English. They had earlier been translated into English in 1859 by an Englishman, Edward Fitzgerald. Till then, poetry lovers all over the East had read them in the original language, Persian. Fitzgerald called the collection *The Rubaiyat* and it made Omar Khayyam world famous. The poems became the most translated in history, into over seventy languages.

The 1,000-plus poems were written as sets of two stanzas of two lines each, what is called a quatrain. That's what the word 'rubaiyat' means in Persian! It's like calling the most beautiful novel 'Paragraph'. Karim Emami's name for the collection, *The Wine of Nishapour*, is more appropriate.

Omar Khayyam lived between 1048 and 1131 in Nishapour, in the north-eastern part of present-day Iran. In his lifetime, he was most well known as an astronomer and mathematician, and less famous for his poetry. But down the centuries, his poems, which are filled with references to wine and love, have influenced Persian, Mughal, Arab and Turkish kings, noblemen, artists and poets.

One of the manuscripts used by Fitzgerald for his translations was from Calcutta, obviously once the possession of a poetry-loving (and wine-drinking) Indian prince or nobleman.

Different translators interpret this 11th century poet differently, but many consider Omar Khayyam a Sufi and a mystic. Naturally, this combination must have had a tremendous influence on Mughal princes, many of whom had strong Sufi leanings, a deep interest in mysticism and a weakness for wine!

19   The Red Tent—A Call to Arms

The vast Mughal camp lay spread across the hot plains
of northern India. Salim, seated on his elephant, could
not even see the boundaries of this camp—it seemed to
stretch on beyond the horizon like a massive metropolis,
rather than a one-night stop. Just yesterday, this plain
had been a quiet empty corner of the empire. Overnight
it had turned into a bustling city, which could
nevertheless uproot itself in a day. When the emperor
and his court moved, the entire capital moved with him.

The prince's eyes scanned the camp. He knew his
father's red tent would be at the centre of the camp.
Red was the colour of royalty. The artillery would be
arranged in an avenue leading up to the royal enclosure
and all around, in neat rows, would be the other
noblemen, their servants, tradesmen and stable boys.

Salim had accompanied his father on enough
expeditions to appreciate that a Mughal camp was far
better than a Mughal city. Its planning was perfect. Each
row of tents was so arranged that when a camp packed
up and pitched tent the following day at another place,
it was an exact replica of the previous night's camp. Deep
in thought, the prince's eyes almost missed something

unusual. Suddenly alert, he snapped out of his dreamy mood and looked again at the spread of the camp. Yes, there across to his right he could see his father's magnificent red tent. But strangely, there seemed to be *another* red tent close to his father's! There was only one emperor, and that was Akbar, as Salim had to acknowledge with bitterness. So who was the other nobleman using the emperor's colours on his tent?

Were the rumours true, then? That his father had indeed permitted Daniyal, his younger brother, to use a red tent? Was this the sign that he, Salim, couldn't afford to wait any longer? In his thirties, Salim's health was worse than his robust father's. If he waited any more, he might never get to be king. The red tent was a call to battle. The fiery Mughal blood coursing through Salim's veins responded to that call. He broke out in open rebellion.

For Akbar, it was to be his final battle, one that no father would want to fight, against his own son. It was to drag on over the last four years of his life. Earlier, every time Akbar had ridden out to war, he'd done so with the supreme confidence that he would win. But this was different. If he fought and defeated the 'enemy', in this case his own rebel son, he'd have won the battle but lost his son. Worse, if his son died in battle, Akbar's entire life's work would lie in ruins. To this most admired of kings, his sense of failure as a father and the very strong possibility of losing this last most important of battles must have overshadowed all his other achievements.

That fatal second red tent sent an electrifying signal to others too. To the courtiers, it indicated that Akbar had totally abandoned Salim and pinned his hopes on Daniyal becoming a good emperor, even though Daniyal's health was much worse than Salim's. He was also far more drunk and not at all as talented as his elder brother Salim. The courtiers now flocked around the younger brother. Even those loyal to Salim deserted him in the face of Akbar's open support to Daniyal. It turned out to be a bad bet on the part of Akbar and his courtiers, because before Daniyal could be crowned emperor, he died.

It looked like Akbar had no choice but to crown Salim. But there soon emerged a powerful faction in court that backed Salim's son, Khusrav, to be made emperor. The succession crisis now pitched two fathers against their sons—Akbar against Salim, and Salim against Khusrav.

The camp followers

One has to admire the unimaginable arrangements that went into moving a Mughal camp. During Akbar's time, and later under Jahangir and his son Shah Jahan's military escapades, discipline was maintained and this vast moving city of over 4,00,000 people worked like a well-oiled machine.

To begin with, the zenana also moved with the king. So naturally, every nobleman travelled with his own harem too. That increased the number of servants and attendants tenfold. Feeding such a large moving population was possible only because the tradesmen and those from the bazaar, too, packed up and moved.

Akbar's military horsemen alone numbered 1,00,000. Then there were war elephants and pack animals like mules, camels, oxen and transport elephants. These amounted to over 2,00,000! The emperor's luggage comprised a double set of *everything*. As soon as one camp was set up and the emperor settled in, an advance party of scouts went ahead to the next camp site to set up the emperor's red tent and erect the wooden paddock around the royal enclosure, so that when the emperor arrived, his comfort at the new camp site was assured.

Akbar's arrangements included an elephant-drawn set of mobile toilets. He also travelled overland with a boat. This was set on wheels and towed in case the royal party had to cross a river anywhere along the journey.

The Camel Bank

A military expedition could take years, so a king had to be prepared for anything. It was important that funds were close at hand. Akbar travelled with his closely guarded 'mobile banking unit'—a set of sturdy camels! Over 200 camels were each loaded with 480 pounds of silver coins. Another 100 camels carried gold of the same weight.

To keep the emperor, his family and the noblemen entertained musicians, dancers, acrobats and other performers followed the camp. Naturally the brave deeds on the battlefield needed to be recorded every day so a battalion of scribes and calligraphers stood ready. Akbar's renowned artists used the outdoors as an opportunity to study plants and animals in their natural settings. Whatever could be found in the famous bazaars of any of the great

Mughal capitals—Delhi, Lahore, Agra or Fatehpur Sikri—could be found at a Mughal camp. Even jewellery, paintings, cosmetics and perfumes! The Mughals travelled in style.

But there were times when the sheer number of camp followers resulted in defeat in battle. In one of Humayun's worst defeats at the hands of Sher Shah at Kanauj, the clever Afghan surrounded the thousands of Mughal camp followers, driving them into the battle-ready Mughal army. With the clear formations of the mounted cavalry battalions, the foot soldiers and the artillery forces all disrupted, these military units couldn't operate as they were trained to and chaos prevailed. Humayun was defeated by the crush of his own camp followers.

20 🐘 A Delicate Game of Chess

After over fifteen years of distrust and tension between Salim and Akbar, it finally seemed like Akbar had given up arms. The king, renowned for his bravery in war, his bloodthirsty shikar expeditions, his tendency to rush into the thick of battle, suddenly wanted no part in it. However provocatively Salim behaved, tempting and taunting his father in order to draw him into battle and settle the succession issue by the sword, Akbar chose to play cool. He indulged his son, wearing him down with diplomatic overtures and choosing every avenue open to him except war.

How much of it was Akbar's own wish to build bridges with his estranged son, and how much was due to the clever, gentle, yet firm intervention of the powerful royal ladies, will never be known. But Hamida Banu Begum, the first lady of the empire, would surely not have allowed her beloved son and equally beloved grandson to destroy each other over the throne.

In 1599, when Akbar left for the Deccan on one of his last military campaigns, he felt it made sense to keep his restless and resentful son occupied. Salim, who was at Ajmer then, was ordered to proceed on the somehow-never-ending Mewar campaign. Though Akbar had captured Chittor early in his reign and even stormed

Udaipur, Mewar's new capital, the Rana always managed to escape into the arid, forested Aravalli hills. It was a long-running battle in which neither party gained. The Mughals had already acquired all the land worth acquiring from Mewar. Yet, his ability to regularly slip away from Mughal hands rankled. And for the Rana, already impoverished by fighting this endless deadend war against a better armed Mughal army, each fight meant only more losses. Yet if he managed to escape, it vastly enhanced his prestige amongst the Rajputs.

No, Salim certainly didn't want to be sucked into this battle with no end. He was in a hurry and had other plans. Instead he left Ajmer and rushed to Agra, hoping to raid the treasury. He didn't succeed. Before his powerful grandmother could collect herself quickly enough to confront and lecture him, he vanished. He next emerged at Allahabad, took the fort, raided the treasury and set up court as an independent ruler. All of this technically amounted to open rebellion and treason. Both crimes normally earned certain death in Mughal times.

Instead Akbar sent an emissary to Allahabad. Salim's close buddy, Khwaja Muhammed Sharif had been fighting by Akbar's side in the Deccan. The father hoped that their mutual friend could help Salim give up his silly notions about a second court. But when Sharif reached Allahabad, Salim convinced him to join his court.

In 1601, Akbar returned from the Deccan but chose not to react to Salim's rebellion. When Salim tried to force matters by riding from Allahabad to Agra at the head of a 30,000-strong army, Akbar kept his cool and Salim was forced to retreat. Even at this advanced stage of Salim's reckless rebellion, Akbar chose to forgive his son and appoint him as governor of Bengal. Again, Salim refused to take up his assigned post. Instead he began minting coins in his own name and even had the cheek to send them to his father for his opinion on their artistic quality!

This time, Akbar chose his only surviving friend, Abul Fazl, to play go-between. It was unfortunate for the emperor that all his dear friends and great statesmen had died before him. Raja Todar Mal, his legendary finance minister, or Raja Birbal, his closest friend, would have been eminently suited to resolve this delicate yet urgent problem between father and son. Unfortunately, Abul Fazl and Salim disliked each other. So as Abul Fazl travelled to Allahabad, Salim had him assassinated.

The death of his close friend shattered Akbar. He seemed to give up. It was time for the ladies to move fast and this they did with incredible success. Salima Begum, Salim's beloved stepmother, set off to Allahabad. There she bullied, berated and bundled the rebellious prince on to an elephant Akbar had specially sent, and brought him back to Agra. Close to the city, Hamida Banu came out to receive her grandson and take him to her mansion. While courtiers and bazaar gossips spread wild rumours about rebellion, treason and the appropriate retaliation, the grand old lady was subtly telling the public that this was a family matter that would be settled accordingly. A relieved Akbar set out to meet his son and their reunion was an emotional one. All was forgiven. Salim's four-year-long rebellion was erased as father and son embraced.

It seemed like Akbar had won his last battle after all, without firing a shot. But there still remained another enemy the old king needed to combat—alcohol.

The Mughal weakness for wine

The Mughals loved living life to the full. They explored and enjoyed every art, craft and sport. And wine just seemed to be the natural accompaniment to their legendary evenings of impromptu poetry composition, art appreciation and musical performances. Babur's own father often offered wine to him, which he refused. Later, as Babur wandered through the courts of his Timurid cousins from Badakshan, Kabul, Kandahar and finally Herat, he was sorely tempted to lose himself in the wine parties his cousins seemed to revel in. Eventually, in his thirties, leading a more settled life in Kabul, he took to wine.

For fifteen years he enjoyed the spirit. Then, after his victory against Ibrahim Lodi at Panipat, and just prior to his battle against the Rajputs at Khanua, Babur swore off liquor. The vast stock of highland wines that he'd carried with him from Kabul was poured down a well, as an offering for help in battle.

But once Hindustan was his, and he'd settled into semi-retirement, Babur took to wine again. Yet Babur never let it interfere with his role as king and military leader.

His son Humayun, unfortunately, was not able to control his drinking. A lot of this king's achievements in battle, science and in administration were nullified by his

prolonged drinking bouts. Of Humayun's two sons, the younger Mohammed Hakim became an alcoholic and died from drinking. Akbar, who himself didn't take to drink, had three sons who all shared a weakness for alcohol. The two younger sons, Murad and Daniyal, died very early from excessive alcohol, and Prince Salim only just escaped following them to an early grave.

21 An Elephantine Tussle

At a grand public reception, Akbar and Salim embraced and the father heaped honours and gifts upon his son. But the moment the last guest had left the hall, the old father grabbed Salim and slapped him. Not once, but a number of times! Time was running out for the family. Couldn't Salim see that? Why wasn't he giving up his wine?

While Salim had given up ideas of rebellion and had reconciled himself to waiting out his time to become king, he just couldn't stop drinking. Daniyal had recently died a slow, miserable and extremely painful death, with the last words on his lips being a prayer for wine. Hamida Banu, Akbar's mother and legendary peace-maker, had died in her seventy-seventh year. There were very few options open to Akbar so he gambled on a drastic choice.

Salim, for all the public show of father-son bonhomie, was put under house arrest. Akbar was determined that wine wouldn't steal away this last son of his. Raja Salivahan, a famous physician, was summoned and Salim placed in his care. The year dragged on for poor Salim under the strict watch of Akbar, the careful diet of Raja Salivahan and a complete ban on drinking, opium and any other possible addiction. Finally Akbar's gamble paid off. At the end of it, Salim emerged a new man. His father had truly managed a miracle.

But just when it seemed that Akbar's last days would be peaceful, trouble cropped up again. Akbar's favourite grandson Khusrav, Salim's eldest son, also wanted to be king. He was old enough, had tremendous public popularity and came without a twenty-year-old record of a drinking problem. Most importantly, he had powerful backers. Like his father, he too was the son of a Rajput princess from a powerful Rajput family. His maternal uncle, Raja Man Singh, was very close to Akbar. His father-in-law was Aziz Koka, Akbar's much-loved foster brother. Akbar too loved him dearly.

As Akbar lay ill from a stomach ailment that was once again suspected to be a case of poisoning, the supporters of Salim and Khusrav began putting pressure on the dying king. It was more than he could bear in his weak condition. He was desperate to settle the issue quickly before he lost consciousness, yet in a manner that seemed impartial. The king, who all his life held reason above religion, and had mocked at the superstitions of all religions, began to look around for some 'omen' to guide him in making a choice. To be fair to Akbar, it must have broken his heart to be forced to choose between a son and a grandson.

In the midst of this crisis, Akbar decided to let the elephants decide! Yes, unbelievably, the heir to the Mughal throne was decided by a pair of elephants—Salim's elephant versus Khusrav's elephant. Salim had more going for him because the Chugtai elders had already held a council and rejected Khusrav's claim to the throne. But Akbar was not convinced that Salim's 'cure' from alcoholism would last more than a few months.

If Akbar was looking for a sign from the elephant battle, he got it loud and clear. A dreadful fight broke out between the supporters of Salim and Khusrav, a sad prophetic prelude to a father-son battle that would continue long after Akbar's death and would only end when Salim imprisoned and blinded his own son.

Salim's elephant emphatically defeated Khusrav's, causing more unpleasant deathbed scenes between the old king and his favourite grandson.

On 21 October 1605, a sad, dying Akbar had his son Salim crowned emperor by his bedside. He was invested with a ceremonial robe made for the occasion. Akbar's turban was placed on Salim's head according to Chugtai custom, and Akbar's dagger slipped into his scabbard.

Four days later, one of India's greatest rulers died.

The way to an emperor's heart . . .

. . . was on an elephant! Of all animals, Akbar was passionate about elephants. He did keep 20,000 pigeons, hundreds of which were trained as carriers. His menagerie included 12,000 deer, an auspicious 101 of which roamed around the palace. He loved dogs and maintained a large kennel. Before he gave it up, he'd especially enjoyed hunting along with a trained cheetah (he had 1,000 of them!). His

favourite hunting mate was a cheetah called Madan Kali, and it was honoured just like other Mughal noblemen; it had kettledrums beating ahead of it announcing its arrival, much like Raja Todar Mal, Abul Fazl and other high-ranking courtiers! But if anybody wanted to win favour with Akbar, all he needed to do was gift the emperor a prize elephant. Neighbouring rajas who wanted to be on good terms with the powerful Mughal court knew about this and so Akbar's elephant stable was full with 'gifts' from across India.

In his young days of daredevilry, Akbar used to mount an elephant by climbing up its trunk, stepping on to its tusks and hoisting himself on to its back! He even used to leap on to the backs of charging elephants from treetops or balconies.

Elephant fights were a favourite spectator sport of the king. Two animals that were evenly matched would be selected to fight, each with two mahouts on their backs. They'd fight across a five-foot thick wall and the game was up either if one animal chased away the other or if the wall was broken.

22 🐘 A True Mughal

Akbar, the great emperor, died a troubled man. He had lost two sons and a brother to wine; and he'd just crowned another not-so-reliable son as king. But in spite of all the years of hard drinking and fooling around, when the chips were down, Prince Salim proved to be every bit his father's son. As Jahangir, he ruled for twenty-two years, during which the Mughal empire was at peace, with its neighbours, that is. Within the family, trouble did erupt, but even that, Jahangir, whom everyone assumed to be a weakling, dealt with decisively. In particular, Jahangir's handling of his son Shah Jahan's rebellions were swift and effective.

Jahangir inherited the best of his father's traits—Akbar's open mind and tolerance for all religions. So on that count, Hindustan continued to be that rare country (probably the only one in the world, at that time) where people of all faiths lived together in peace, *as equals*. Unlike Akbar, he wasn't particularly interested in Christianity, though he allowed the Portuguese Jesuits to go about their church building and conversion (he even gave them a pension from the treasury to do so). His interests were purely in Sufiism and the Vedanta branch of Hinduism.

Another passion he shared with Akbar was art. Jahangir collected paintings from all parts of the world, and the Mughal artists under his supervision created masterpieces. European art that came into India with the new trading colonies of the Portuguese, English and Dutch inspired local miniaturists to explore perspective, light and depth in a way they'd never attempted earlier. Today, miniatures from Jahangir's reign are rated the best from the Mughal school of painting.

Mughal miniatures were often not the product of one artist. An action scene could be painted by someone who could depict action well, with the faces left blank. This would be filled out by the 'face expert', and completed by someone else who was good with borders. As Jahangir himself boasted in his journal, he could point out the work of every artist in his atelier! Jahangir claimed that even if every face in a miniature were painted by a separate artist, he would be able to spot each one's style.

A major development under Jahangir was the scale at which Mughal art grew. Jahangir seemed to find the scale of a miniature too limiting. Unlike earlier, when artists only worked as illustrators of manuscripts, Jahangir taught his subjects to enjoy art for its own sake. He far preferred larger, stand-alone paintings, in the European tradition, and encouraged his artists to think big.

Artists now had a much larger canvas to work on. The walls of the palace became theirs. Europeans report seeing frescos of the Madonna, beautifully painted behind the Mughal throne, right beside portraits of Jahangir himself, along with other Mughal bigwigs.

From his great grandfather, Babur, Jahangir inherited his love for nature. Gardening was a passion with him and his scientific interest and study of plants and animals were well ahead of his time. Like Babur, he fancied himself a poet. Unique amongst the Mughals, he was an acclaimed calligraphist. And like his great grandfather, he too wrote a journal. For a period of twelve years, he recorded all his thoughts, observations and what happened. Jahangir had been a good student as a boy, unlike his father (who couldn't write and had to depend on biographers to record his reign). The journal, now known as the *Jahangir-nama*, reveals a side of him that no biographer could have captured . . . or dared to record! Like the *Babur-nama*, written by Babur himself, and the *Humayun-nama*, written by Humayun's sister Gulbadan Begum, it's a view of the spectacular Mughal court from the best seat in the theatre—the throne!

Adding chillies to an already spicy diet

Christianity and European Art were not the only imports brought into India by the Portuguese. In Akbar's time itself tobacco had been introduced into India and while orthodox Muslim clerics frowned upon this new habit, Akbar seemed to have no problems with his courtiers smoking.

Since Spain and Portugal had colonized South America, apart from tobacco, other South American crops came to India. In case you thought chillies, tomatoes and potatoes were part of our diet since the time of

the Vedas, think again. They came to India on Portuguese ships.

The other important aspect of the Europeans in India was all the journals and records they kept. These are now great additional sources to study the Mughal period.

TRIVIA
TREASURY

Turn the pages to discover more fascinating facts and tantalizing tidbits of history about this legendary life and his world.

WHAT HAPPENED AND WHEN

- **14 February 1483:** Babur was born in Fergana, a small kingdom in Central Asia.
- **9 June 1494:** Twelve-year-old Babur is crowned king when his father, Umar Shaikh Mirza, dies in a landslide that took along a corner of his castle (the dovecote that the pigeon-rearing king had built at the edge of a cliff).
- **1497:** Babur captures Samarkand from his cousin after a siege of seven months.
- **1497 (100 days later):** Loses Samarkand *and* Fergana to nobles who propped up his brother, Jahangir, as a puppet king.
- **1504:** After seven years of wandering about minus a throne, Babur captures Kabul, when his cousin Ulegh Beg Mirza dies, leaving an infant son as heir.
- **April 1526:** First Battle of Panipat, in which 20,000 of Babur's men defeat the 1,00,000-strong army of Afghan king Ibrahim Lodi.
- **August 1526:** Babur defeats the Rajput confederacy and their Afghan allies at Khanua.
- **26 December 1530:** Babur dies after a short illness.
- **30 December 1530:** Twenty-three-year-old Humayun is crowned king. Of Babur's Indo-Afghan kingdom, Humayun gets the Indian territories;

brother Kamran gets Kabul and Kandahar; and Hindal and Askari get smaller fiefs.

- **1534–36**: Humayun's expansion phase begins when he captures Gujarat, sending local king Bahadur Shah fleeing for his life to the island Diu. But by the time Humayun returns to Delhi, twenty months later, he loses Gujarat and Malwa, again.
- **1537–39**: Battles are fought between Humayun and Sher Shah over Bihar. Humayun loses and returns to Agra.
- **1540**: In a battle for the Mughal throne, Sher Shah defeats Humayun and the Mughal king flees west.
- **1541**: Humayun marries Hamida Banu Begum in Sind, while on the run.
- **15 October 1542**: Akbar is born in a Rajput fort in Umarkot.
- **July 1543**: With no support from his brothers, Humayun leaves Hindustan for Persia.
- **1544**: Hamida Banu Begum and Humayun leave baby Akbar behind and spend a year in Persia, enjoying the good life under the Shah's protection.
- **1545**: Humayun returns to attack Kandahar with Persian troops; defeats Kamran and takes Kabul too. Is reunited with son Akbar.
- **22 May 1545**: Sher Shah dies of burns in Kalinjar.
- **1556**: Humayun crosses into India and captures Delhi, Agra and his lost kingdom.
- **1556**: Humayun dies in Delhi after falling down the stairs.
- **February 1556**: Akbar is crowned king while

camping out in Kalanaur, Punjab, with Biram Khan as regent.

- **November 1556**: Second Battle of Panipat, Mughals under Biram Khan beat Afghans led by General Hemu.
- **1560**: Akbar breaks away from under Biram Khan's control.
- **1561**: Akbar conquers Malwa.
- **1564**: The Gond kingdom is added to Mughal territory.
- **1566**: Battles for Rajput kingdoms begin, with a campaign in Mewar.
- **1573**: Akbar conquers Gujarat.
- **1581**: Marches to Kabul, chasing out younger brother Mohammed Hakim and hands over control of the region to sister Bakhtunissa Begum.
- **1582**: Akbar's creed of living in religious harmony, Din-i-Ilahi, is launched.
- **1604**: Akbar's mother, Hamida Banu Begum, dies.
- **25 October 1605**: Akbar dies and Prince Salim (Jahangir) is crowned emperor.
- **1606**: Jahangir's eldest son Khusrav rebels and is jailed for fourteen years.
- **1611**: Jahangir marries the widowed Nur Jahan.
- **1621**: Prince Khurram (later Shah Jahan), adds the Deccan kingdoms to the Mughal empire.
- **1622**: Khurram rebels against his father.
- **1626**: An eight-month-long coup by army commander Mahabat Khan has Jahangir and Nur Jahan held as prisoners.
- **1627**: Months after the end of the coup, Jahangir dies while out on a shikar.

MEANWHILE IN THE REST OF THE WORLD

The period of Akbar's life and reign in India stands out even more dramatically as a haven of tolerance, when compared to what was happening in the rest of the world. The 16th and 17th centuries saw the greatest expansion in slave trade, where Portuguese, Spanish and Dutch ships transported kidnapped Africans to the Caribbeans, South America and North America to work on sugar plantations and mines.

The horrors of colonization came to Asia relatively later, but Europeans had already decimated and subjugated large parts of Mexico, what we now know as the United States and South America.

In 1556 China, a vast country of contrasts like India, experienced the worst earthquake in recorded history at Shaanxhi province. Records reveal that over 8,30,000 people died—three-fourth of the population that lived within a 500-mile radius from the epicentre. The death count was so high because people lived in dugouts on the face of cliffs, called yaodongs.

In Europe, in 1564, artists, scientists and architects were exploring new ways of looking at things. One archetypical Renaissance man, Michelangelo, had just died. Apart from hundreds of works of art, he was best known as the man who'd painted the ceiling of the Sistine Chapel in Rome, the sculptor of the famous 'Pieta' (Mary with the dead body of Jesus) and David, and eventually, the designer of the dome of St. Paul's Basilica in Rome (the largest in the world).

In India, the scourge that haunted the land was famine, either due to lack of rain or because of incessant wars that ruined standing crops. In Europe, another problem was the plague. While London witnessed the epidemic return every ten years, in 1575 the city of Venice was nearly destroyed by the disease.

In Japan, the Portuguese and Dutch had arrived, setting up trading colonies in southern Nagasaki. By the early 1600s, over 3,00,000 Japanese had converted to Christianity, including a famous warlord, who even sent a delegation to Pope Gregory XIII in Rome.

Along with Christianity came guns, which the Japanese soon copied, adapted and manufactured in such large numbers that in the early 17th century the militia of the Japanese warlords carried the most guns in the world!

AKBAR LIVES ON ...

- The Red Fort at Agra has a number of buildings from Akbar's era. The main entrance to the fort is called the Akbari Darwaza. A building that now lies in ruins within the fort is the Akbari Mahal. The Jahangiri Mahal, though its name suggests otherwise, was built by Akbar, probably for the women in his family, since there are no exterior windows on the lower storey.

- The abandoned ghost town of Fatehpur Sikri is an embodiment of Akbar. It showcases his bold artistic vision. It broke away from Persian and West Asian architectural designs and used Indian building material, designs and techniques mainly from Rajasthan, Gujarat and Central India.
- At Sikander, off the Delhi–Agra highway, is Akbar's tomb. It was designed during his lifetime and considerable work had been done before his death. Jahangir supervised its completion.
- After the heat and dust of the Delhi–Agra highway, Wikipedia is a good quiet place to trace Akbar's life! Google for 'Gulbadan Begum' and you will find both excerpts and the entire text of the *Humayun-nama* which covers Akbar's childhood. Abul Fazl's *Akbar-nama* can also be read online.
- Two movies made right after India got independence went on to become big hits. They were both based on a legend of Prince Salim's love for a slave girl, Anarkali. The story plays out against the backdrop of Akbar's disapproval. *Anarkali* was made in 1953, with actress Bina Rai playing Anarkali and Pradeep Kumar playing Prince Salim. It was the highest grossing film that year. But it was *Mughal-e-Azam*, released in 1960, that broke all box office records (till *Sholay* appeared decades later). In this film, Akbar is played by Prithviraj Kapoor (Kareena Kapoor's great granddad!) and Salim by Dilip Kumar. Most of the film had already been shot in black and white by director K. Asif, when colour film got introduced. So since his financers

refused to let him reshoot the entire film in colour, he shot key song sequences and the climax in colour!

- Among children, Akbar is best remembered as the partner of Birbal in the innumerable 'Akbar and Birbal' stories. Amar Chitra Katha has a set of five comics of just this king–and–jester pair. You can also read Puffin's *Akbar and Birbal* by Amita Sarin.

BOOKS TO READ

Here are some books I read while writing this book:

1. *The Oxford History of India* by Vincent A. Smith (Oxford University Press, USA, 1981, 4th edition)
2. *Emperors of the Peacock Throne* by Abraham Eraly (Penguin Books India, 1997)
3. *The Mughal World* by Abraham Eraly (Penguin Books India, 2007)
4. *The Concise Encyclopaedia of Islam* by Cyril Glasse (Stacey International, 2003)
5. *Royal Mughal Ladies and Their Contribution* by Soma Mukherjee (Gyan Publishing, 2001)
6. *Our Oriental Heritage*, from Will Durant's *The Story of Civilization* series (Simon and Schuster, 1935)
7. *King of the World: the Padshahnama, an imperial Mughal manuscript from the Royal Library, Windsor Castle*, Milo Cleveland and Ebba Koch (Azimuth Editions, 1997)